Foreword by Dr. Robert Christie, (Retired), Faculty of Outdoor Recreation, Lakehead University, Thunder Bay, Canada.

ISBN 0-9694132-0-3
Printed by Skyway Printing, Hanover, Ontario

ACKNOWLEDGEMENTS

Many people provided valuable assistance towards the development of this book, and to them I extend my gratitude and appreciation. At the risk of omitting someone, I would like to thank Bill McKenzie; Frank Yamich, Chief Instructor, Survival in the Bush, Inc.; David Arama, Assistant Instructor; Joseph Commodari, Assistant Instructor; and Don Johnston, Searchmaster, Lakehead Search and Rescue Unit.

A special thanks to Filomena, my wife, for inspiring and illustrating this book.

Credits: Snow Cave, Figure-4 Dead fall, Stick Method of Direction Finding, Birch Bark Goggles, Fire Bow: David Arama.

Snow Shelter, Fish Hooks, Harpoon, Kudlik: Frank Yamich.

Vehicular Survival kit, Search and Rescue: Lakehead Search and Rescue Unit.

Shock: Robert Donaghy.

Potassium Permanganate, Gut Twine: Ken Dudzinski.

Dressing for the Outdoors: Joseph Commodari.

Search and Rescue Statistics: Ontario Provincial Police.

Sketches by Filomena Ferri.

Revisions: Grade 7 students, Mother Teresa School, Walkerton

Final editing: Doug Wainscott

With the help of more than 200 photos and sketches, Gino Ferri shows you how to build practical shelters using only what nature has to offer...to identify and utilize edible, herbal, and useful greenery...to start fires without matches...to obtain and prepare insects and wild game as food...to fashion aboriginal tools...to use a vehicle as a survival device...to trail blaze...to construct distress signals...as well as a host of other related wilderness survival skills.

Using human ingenuity and resourcefulness as guidelines, this book presents a practical, common sense approach to survival.

Individuals who understand the stress, pain, and hardships confronting the stranded victim will gain a deeper insight and respect for the wilderness survivor.

One such victim, a graduate of Gino's survival course, was stranded in a remote region of the Yukon. Says he "...I used his advice and training to live off the land for seven days before help arrived. His teaching methods may be unconventional, but they work. I'm living proof..."

The Psychology of Wilderness Survival contains information which may be invaluable in dealing with a sudden wilderness emergency situation. This knowledge, mastered prior to venturing into the bush, could be life-saving.

We do not claim that our techniques will ensure survival. This depends on the circumstances and the individual(s) concerned. They will, however, enhance the victim's chances of living.

Some methods described in this book should be practiced under the direction of qualified instructors. Misuse of any techniques could result in personal or property damage, for which we disclaim any liability.

TO BELLA, WITH LOVE

| TOPIC | PAGE |

Wilderness survival students, Humber College, Toronto, Ontario

(e)

Reaction to the initial edition of *The Psychology of Wilderness Survival:*

"Absolutely, the most comprehensive book ever written on wilderness survival.

Recommended by the Ontario Federation of Anglers & Hunters as must reading for anyone who enters the wilderness. Not simply a 'how to' book. This is the 'Bible' on wilderness survival."

. . . *Angler & Hunter* magazine.

All copies of the first edition were sold out within two weeks of publication.

THE PSYCHOLOGY OF WILDERNESS SURVIVAL

FOREWORD

Not too long ago, a young hunter was disoriented and unable to find his way back to his car in an area of northern Ontario. He was expected to meet his hunting partner at 2 p.m. Eight days later, he walked out of the woods many kilometres west of where he started. He had travelled in a westerly direction because he knew a north-south road was located there. A vague knowledge of the sun's position in the sky was his primary navigation aid. While lost, he experienced fear, hunger, thirst, cold and hallucinations. His feet were frost nipped on his last night in the woods, the coldest night of his ordeal. The hunter was lightly clothed, carried a few paper matches that became wet and useless in the rain, and had no compass. He drank water from a variety of sources, ate a few berries, some plant leaves and parts of a raw duck that he had shot. Each night, he had constructed a crude shelter and covered himself with a pile of leaves or boughs from conifers. He was unaware that his route was running parallel to an east-west road located just a few kilometres north of his erratic path. Daily, he walked further away from the area being scoured by search and rescue teams working on the ground and in the air. If he had "Stayed Put" when he first realized he was lost, he would have been rescued within 24 hours. Initially, he panicked and walked rapidly through the bush until it was almost dark. Finally, he began to analyze the situation and initiate actions that enabled him to survive.

In the fall of 1984, an American pilot crash landed his plane near the rugged north shore of Lake Superior. He survived the crash without apparent injury. However, two weeks later, his body was found on the shores of the lake a few kilometres from the crash site. He died of hypothermia an undetermined number of days after the crash. He was dressed in light clothing. The pilot had survival training but there were few signs that he used it. He had not constructed a shelter or built a fire. Temperatures fluctuated above and below freezing and there were periods of cold rain and snow during his ordeal. On the night of the crash, he had left at dusk for a 500 kilometre flight into an area that was experiencing bad weather. There was no radio transmitter aboard the plane. He was unfamiliar with the area.

Neither of these survival ordeals should have occurred. Lack of preparation and bad judgement contributed to both situations. Neither person had adequate knowledge of their area. Neither person was carrying essential equipment and clothing that would have provided for their needs in case of an emergency. Still, both could have survived but only one did. The warmer temperatures and the use of shelters, apparently, were the difference.

Survival is a no-nonsense situation. A person should be prepared to cope with the particular factors that must be faced in each specific situation. Individuals should know key principles and be able to apply them in a variety of circumstances. There are no pat answers that can be taught; therefore, each situation must be analyzed and dealt with according to the circumstances. In addition to being proficient in some of the essential survival skills, individuals should also know something about the area they may be required to survive in, the climate and weather, flora and fauna, escape routes, search and rescue practices and procedures for the area, and also be able to function effectively under condition of stress and isolation.

The mind is a most essential component in the formula for survival. To be prepared means to be able to cope with encounters with fear, cold, heat, wetness, injury, and insects and still make sound decisions. It is a battle of the mind and body against the elements.

If you were in a survival situation, how would you react? Could you control fear and panic? Would you be mentally prepared to analyze your situation, establish a logical course of action and do the things that would help you to survive? Do you know and practice the basic skills that are most essential? Would you have the will to survive?

Unfortunately, the term "survival" has been greatly overused, and consequently abused, in promoting outdoor programs. The term has been glamorized and misrepresented to attract people. In addition, many "arm-chair" authors have written books and articles on survival, but have never practiced what they have written. As a result, many people believe they are able to cope with survival situations. Life threatening situations usually are not encountered with sleeping bags, food, camping equipment, tents or permanent shelters.

Survival education should focus upon mental preparation to deal with stress and the proficiency in essential survival skills. Some skills can be useful as psychological props but in actuality do not contribute to the survival of the individual. Shelter building and firemaking are two skills that can make a difference. Locating and utilizing drinking water is essential. Knowing how to signal for help can assist searchers or others to know where you are and that you need help. A person can live for weeks without food. Foraging and eating many wild edibles can frequently be "counter productive" to survival and should be dealt with accordingly. When faced with a life threatening situation, a person must be able to exert self-control and do the things necessary to stay alive.

Gino Ferri has devoted much of his life to the study and practice of survival education. He has acquired knowledge and skills under the leadership of experts in the field, including outdoorsmen and natives who retain the practices of their culture. On many occasions he has entered the bush equipped only with a few tools and the clothing on his back to "survive" for varying lengths of time, ranging from days to months. In addition, he has researched the survival field extensively, including the examination of living skills dating back to the cave man. Throughout this, the researcher has acquired an extensive knowledge of the psychological factors associated with survival situations. While already proficient with a broad variety of survival skills, he has a continuing desire to expand his learning about survival in different environments. His research and wide experience are reflected in the book.

Survival is staying alive. Survival situations will continue to occur as hunters, hikers, campers and many others find themselves lost or stranded. Survival education should help people to know how to avoid life-threatening situations and prepare them to live through stressful and unexpected events. It is more than useful to know how to function effectively with or without essential items of equipment and clothing. It can happen to any one of us.

Dr. R. Christie, Director,
Faculty of Physical Education &
Outdoor Recreation,
Lakehead University,
THUNDER BAY, Ontario, Canada.
(Retired)

A survival student "fishes" for minnows and leeches using a sock "net" and an unravelled scarf for line. Practicality is the hallmark of intelligent survival training.

A WORD TO THE READER:

Wilderness survival situations are normally unplanned, highly stressful events where factors are controlled not through planning, but most often through improvisation. Hence, most survival situations occur without much advance warning; a hunter is separated from his party, and becomes lost in thick bush without any gear, matches, or food; an avid fisherman dumps his canoe in foaming rapids; a trapper's snow machine suddenly breaks through thin ice...These are now potentially desperate survival situations.

Survival implies a driving will to live, regardless of the necessary actions required to accomplish this goal.   True, although any available equipment undoubtedly facilitates the survivor's stay in the wilderness, possessing a strong will to live does not eminate from any amount of spiffy gear, preppy survival kits, or fashionable camping supplies. Instead, it derives from the human intellect! This book attempts to address the mind, not stylish gimmicks.

Traditionally, survival manuals have listed, expounded, and encouraged readers to develop all sorts of devices appropriate to various emergencies. One is advised to construct deadfalls requiring an engineering degree to complete; fashion next to useless shelters; or propose activities, such as raft building, that are completely impractical in a survival situation.

To some extent, we will include a number of food procurement techniques in this manual; however, for a non-traditional reason! Research in the field of wilderness survival clearly illustrates that the chief danger facing the survivor is the almost uncontrollable urge to wander aimlessly throughout the wilderness, thereby wantonly wasting precious calories and energy. Besides offering the victim some faint hope of capturing game, the construction of deadfalls, harpoons, and snares, in our opinion, serves to keep the survivor occupied, and close to his shelter. In so doing, he rations his energy, is safe being close to the confines of his "home" area, and offers Search and Rescue Units the opportunity to concentrate their efforts in one general area.

Furthermore, we advise the victim to refrain from potentially dangerous activities such as gathering plants as a food source; this activity usually consumes more calories (and energy) than is obtained by eating foraged plants; and consuming unknown vegetation could prove disastrous to the victim. Unless stranded in the midst of a walnut or oak grove, an extensive berry patch, or a similar food supply, we suggest that the victim remain close to his shelter, and drink plenty of water. In this regard, even though we highlight an extensive list of edible plants, we refuse to equate a pleasant day's foraging activities to the desperate mental anguish facing the wilderness survivor; we do not use survival as a gimmick to sell our programmes.

Today's marketplace is flooded with a wide variety of wilderness survival manuals, books, and magazines. The following four basic philosophical viewpoints differentiate this jungle of texts:

1. Armchair Survivor Mentality: these authors view survival from a neat, clean, somewhat academic standpoint, applying a logical, urban rationale to a wilderness environment. Such writers recommend practices which seem sound on paper (or in one's living room), but spell potential disaster in the wilderness. Members of this category believe they can successfully tear apart a beaver dam to catch fish, construct lakeworthy rafts, or set up sophisticated and complicated deadfall...all with a penknife!

2. High-Tech Camping Philosophy: followers of this viewpoint do not condone any destruction of the wilderness, even under survival conditions. This group does not accept the killing of trees and animals for purposes of survival training. Authors in this category often treat survival in a somewhat flippant matter, firmly believing in their fancy, sophisticated high-tech camping gear. Some of their suggested survival hints includes catching fish by tickling their bellies; sleeping directly on snow; and digging deep pits, in boreal forests, to trap large game. To the realistic survival instructor, these suggestions are laughable!

3. Spiritual Re-awakening School of Thought: these high priests of survival denounce all forms of tampering with the wilderness, seriously believing that no insect, tree, or animal should be harmed, under most circumstances. Proponents of this philosophical viewpoint, strongly influenced by native religions, surmise that the victim gains spiritual strength from watching and appreciating his surroundings, thereby enabling him to survive. This group, it seems, has yet to discover mosquitoes and blackflies.

   Proponents of these philosophies tend to diffuse the ugly aspects related to wilderness survival. Instead, their commentaries read more like pleasant camping trips than survival ordeals. Not surprisingly, these groups vehemently attack and debase the following realistic, if somewhat harsh view point.....

4. Do Anything to Survive Mentality: this philosophy advises anyone unfortunate enough to become mired in a survival situation to forsake urban values and do whatever needs doing to live. This includes remaining stationary; not wantonly wasting precious calories on foolishly planned activities such as chasing fish, constructing condominiums, or wandering through the wilderness seeking a vision quest.

Authors of this school of thought are rare indeed, since wilderness survival is not exploited as a selling or advertising gimmick; instead, they suggest that survival, being a stressful situation, causes people to react in an unpredictable, sometimes ugly, manner. Stripped of his thin civilized veneer, the victim is faced with fearful surroundings, unknown feelings, deprivations, fickle elements, insensitive and unrelenting insects, and a seemingly hostile, unforgiving environment.

This is Wilderness Survival! There is nothing glamorous or pretty about this deadly situation. Precipitated by unforseen circumstances, emergencies, or just plain bad luck, survival is a highly stressful situation. We discuss these elements to some depth, since, quite simply, this is wilderness survival. By concentrating on the victim's mental aspects, we utilize the human mind to the fullest. Survival, in our opinion, is an attitude, a mental set that must be controlled and utilized.

This philosophy, quite naturally, is not for everyone. Only you, the reader, can effectively decide your own personal preferences. It might assure you to know, dear reader, that the suggestions, advice and comments made in this book have been tried and tested ... under survival conditions.

Finally this book was put together in an effort to provide a manual for taking part in realistic wilderness survival programmes; contents are a direct result of reviewing statistics involving 2,600 victims stranded in the bush.

Ironically, many instructors who teach realistic wilderness survival courses encounter severe criticism from some members of today's urbanized society.

WILDERNESS SURVIVAL

Cruel is the land most people admire
Yet they never experience
The true hardships
And struggles which are in continuum
Through her entity.
To say that man is superior within her grasp
Is a complete fallacy,
A farce.
Man's attitudes and appearances
Change so drastically after dealing
With you, Mother Nature.
The Woman is beautiful and enticing, yet
Hidden sorrow and quiet pain and hardened reality
Are released when one of us is trapped
By your unexpected and uncaring ways.
You neither help nor hurt us
But you do both in a very defined way.
Those who respect you are wise.
Those who deny you are foolish,
For you are the birth of our true selves.

Mike Sillet, Student,
Resource Technician Training Program,
Goose Bay, Labrador.

Written following a three-week wilderness survival training session in the vicinity of Northwest River, Labrador.

"MAN'S CAPACITIES HAVE NEVER BEEN MEASURED; NOR ARE WE TO JUDGE WHAT WE CAN DO BY ANY PRECEDENTS, SO LITTLE HAS BEEN TRIED. WHAT PEOPLE SAY YOU CANNOT DO, YOU TRY AND FIND YOU CAN."

THOREAU

GENESIS: THE SURVIVAL PROGRAMME

Our survival courses are offered by Humber College, Toronto, Canada. In the Autumn of 1977, we began to teach realistic and practical wilderness survival techniques on a year-round basis, with each course structured to provide its own specific areas of concern. For example, during the fall course, the central theme is snares, traps, and deadfalls for small game, since this is a season when these animals are quite active in preparation for winter, and survival shelters aimed at being effective on those cold nights.

The winter survival course concentrates on practical winter shelters (both stone shelters and snow caves) and the special concerns of maintaining body temperature under extreme conditions.

The spring programme focuses on the identification and preparation of edible, useful and herbal greenery, and the seasonal problems of mosquitoes, black flies, deer flies, moose flies, and no-see-ums.

During the spring and summer months, erect shelter in open areas, close to water. This offers some protection from bugs. It also makes the victim more visible to search and rescue parties.

Other topics include wilderness emergency care; skinning and preparing wild game as food; tools and other gear to make at the survival site; fire building, including the use of flint, fire bow, and batteries; poisonous plants to avoid; utilizing a vehicle in an emergency situation; trail blazing; distress signals, as well as a host of other related survival topics.

Students wishing to practice these newly acquired skills have the opportunity to attend our summer simulation course, a nine-day programme held during the month of August. This is a chance to implement all survival skills, including intensively foraging for food. The simulation programme is taught completely in the wilderness, and totally immerses students in a realistic survival atmosphere.

The other courses are divided into two related segments: the theoretical components, and skills required for survival are discussed in a ten-week classroom teaching session; the practical, field experience: two weekend survival outings in the wilds of Northern Ontario. The first weekend is best described as a "soft" survival outing. Students are divided into small groups, with each group assigned to a specific survival area. An instructor is stationed with each group. Participants are expected to put all of their classroom knowledge to full practical use; instructors are on hand to offer assistance when needed. All are encouraged to make full use of their instructors. S(he) may identify edible plants, help with fire-starting and shelter construction, as well as assist with the making of various survival gear (hooks, bark vessels, tri-stands, and cooking racks). On the other hand, instructors are not there

Snails quickly eliminate "plate fright". As days drag on, hunger pains force the survivor to consume anything resembling food.

to do someone's work for him. Survival education implies that each person looks after himself.

Participants may wish to arrive Friday evening or early Saturday morning. In any case, all students must be ready to trek (4-6 km) to the sites by 08:00 hours Saturday morning. The College and its instructors take no responsibility for students arriving late.

Exactly what is expected of the novice during this initial wilderness outing? Since there are anywhere from 5 - 10 participants in each group, each person shares such communal tasks as firewood gathering, foraging, and shelter construction. Otherwise, everyone is pretty much on his own. All should practice what was taught in the classroom:
- various cooking methods and food preparation
- shelter construction
- utilizing edible plants, and
- fire starting techniques.

Should time permit, some people set snares and deadfalls; make utensils; or fashion fishhooks, harpoon, and throwing sticks. Instructors are there to share their expertise with any interested person. It is very easy to lay back and do absolutely nothing - the student's learning will be proportionate to his efforts.

Shelter, cooking, and food preparation skills must be mastered during this outing. Also, it is vital that the survival site be explored. This prepares the student for the next outing - the total survival session. All should trail blaze at all times!

Keep eyes open for natural shelters, edible plants, animal runways and signs, as well as any features which might ensure a more comfortable survival site. Two thoughts should always be at the back of everyone's mind:
1. There is no warm building around. No hotels in the bush!
2. This is not a camping course. Each will soon experience the fact that sleeping bags, axes, pots, pans and tents are sheer items of luxury. All are encouraged to make the best of what is provided by nature.

Once in the field, students are not forced or coerced to practice any survival skills. On the other hand, the instructor certainly helps anyone needing assistance. To some, this approach is a difficult experience; no one telling the student what to do! Each person is his own!

Some participants may buckle in this environment and loudly exclaim - "I HAVE NOTHING TO DO!" Yet, all must keep in mind that the initial trip is geared to "getting your feet wet", so to speak. Otherwise, some might find the drastic change from urban comforts to wilderness survival conditions too much to handle. With this thought in mind, all participants have the option of bringing any gear supplied by us along with his/her own personal equipment.

Remember: what each person brings in, (s)he takes out!

Following are some of the aims for the first outing:
1. discovering- overpacking: clothes, food, equipment
   - lack of proper shelters and bedding
   - improper dress, over or underdressing
2. characteristics of individuals under survival conditions
3. attitudes towards ourselves and others
4. lack of classroom preparation
5. getting to know each other
6. learn from the mistakes made so that they will not be repeated
7. find out why some were cold and uncomfortable, while others were warm
8. discover the level of each student re: wilderness survival skills

Prior to leaving, each group must arrive at a consensus as to when they will leave. Each group must leave as a group; all groups should leave no later than 12:00 hours on Sunday. All groups must notify the instructor that they are leaving. This is imperative.

Following this outing, a detailed classroom discussion takes place, at which time discussion focuses on likes and dislikes, mistakes which were made, good points of the trip, along with the bad ones. As well, a questionnaire will be distributed. These are returned to the instructor as soon as possible.

The second outing is somewhat different. Although participants may arrive Friday night (staying at same spot as before) or Saturday morning; everyone must be at the departure site no later than 08:30 a.m. Here, each team (2 per team - some may wish to solo) chooses individual survival sites; all teams are completely isolated, and must survive using only the contents of their survival kits. This is the peak experience of the course. Students are expected to use every survival skill gleaned from classroom instruction. On Sunday, participants may stay as late as 12:00 hours. However, participants do not leave without informing the instructor. Each team is scheduled to be checked at various times throughout the weekend.

Needless to say, littering has no place in this course. Anything carried in must be carried out.

With regard to felling trees; that is, the trees needed for erecting shelters and making bedding, students must utilize every part of the tree. We remind participants that a certain amount of saplings are needed to effectively teach proper shelter construction skills.

All must remove any snares or deadfalls prior to leaving.

Students suffering from any allergies are required to inform the instructor the nature and extent of their reactions. Any medical problems must also be reported, in writing, no later than the second week of classes.

Drinking alcoholic beverages and/or non-medical use of drugs is not acceptable on any of our outings. Possession is reason enough for immediate dismissal from any of the survival courses.

Finally, participation in both weekend sessions is mandatory.

GUIDELINES: SUGGESTED GEAR FOR WEEKEND TRIPS (MAXIMUM)

1. Jerky or pemmican (100 gm limit)
2. Heavy coat
3. Hat, mitts or gloves
4. Heavy-duty knife
5. Raincoat, poncho type
6. Proper bush clothing
7. Blanket (Winter only)
8. Snowshoes (Winter only)
9. Snare wire
10. Tin can

PROBLEMS: TEACHING SURVIVAL COURSES IN AN URBAN SOCIETY

Due to the realistic nature of our programme, all potential participants must be interviewed by the instructor. At this stage, the details pertaining to the programme are outlined; all questions are answered before anyone attends classes. Some individuals cannot handle or accept segments of the content matter, especially those topics generally not condoned by an urbanized society. Criticism of any realistic survival course falls under four general headings:

CONCEPT OF (UN) ACCLIMATIZATION

Wilderness survival situations have a nasty habit of removing man's artificial body protection and those modern conveniences on which he has become dependent upon to maintain his existence. Once society loses its modern services, the inhabitants must - individually or collectively - cope with an emergency. Heat, water, food, medical aid, and shelter must be acquired. During this time, the survivor is the master of his own destiny.

However, in modern society, man is totally dependent on outside powers to supply him with the necessities of life. We are not in control of our lives! And here lies the problem: we have lost the ability to cope with any adversity. It has been educated out of our knowledge by the prospect of prompt aid and comfort from outside agencies in any type of crisis.

Unacclimatized persons are easy prey to cold, hunger, pain, bugs, and just plain uncomfortable situations. They'll whine if problems, especially those relating to a wilderness setting, aren't immediately looked after. They've become so conditioned to modern lifestyles that living without the comforts of home (heating in winter, air-conditioning in summer) becomes next to impossible. Such people have never been truly hungry or cold, and could never understand the drastic course of action taken by survival instructors to insure that students understand the true meaning of wilderness survival.

PHILOSOPHICAL DIFFERENCES

The four main philosophical viewpoints pertaining to the teaching of wilderness survival, and how some individuals use "wilderness survival" as an advertising or selling gimmick...
- the armchair survivalist mentality;
- the spiritualist-seeker mentality;
- the light-weight camper mentality; and
- the do-anything to survive viewpoint.

These are directly opposed to each other, causing severe problems for the realistic instructor. The first three philosophical viewpoints abstract the ugly aspects of survival, including killing animals, the reactions of some people under stressful situations, and the personal experiences and actions of some survivors.

In our programme, we include these concepts, because, quite simply, some aspects of wilderness survival are not pleasant. Indeed, our guest speakers include victims who suffered the living hell of the Nazi concentration camps.

SYMBOLIC INTERPRETATION: ANIMALS

In an urban society, cats, dogs and other pets, sometimes becoming surrogate children. Usually, animals are given human characteristics, feelings, and emotions. Pets often eat as well as their human masters.

On the contrary, a hunting or survival situation dictates that all animals work for their keep. Few are pets. If so, for a limited time period only. Although respected, animals are bred for work or for meat and usually fed scraps from their master's leftovers. Individuals living under these circumstances live in a wilderness setting, and are usually in tune with the natural environment.

SYMBOLIC INTERPRETATION: MEAT PROCUREMENT

Urban society places the abattoir workers, those that actually slaughter and kill animals, at the bottom of the social scale. The distributer (IGA, Dominion, Loblaws, and local butchers) are somewhat higher on the social ladder. Socially speaking, gourmet cooks are by far the highest and most in demand for social events.
The hunting or survival economy places the procurer of food, the hunter or trapper, highest on the social scale; these are the most important people on the social ladder. They are very much needed to insure the group's survival. The procurer then distributes the meat to underlings who cut up and distribute meat. Cooks are menial labourers, and are the lowest members of society. Occasionally, they are treated as servants.

One notes how these values are at loggerheads with each other, causing almost insurmountable problems for instructors attempting to conduct realistic survival programmes to urbanized individuals.

Our courses dispel the notion of the wilderness as being a romantic utopia. Futhermore, we reject the notion that one's survival depends solely on a survival kit. We stress, at all times, the extreme importance of having a positive mental attitude. If some gear is available, great! Use it! However, if a survival kit is not on hand, our students are taught to use whatever nature has to offer.

Attitudes towards meat procurement and preparation are often major obstacles when dealing with realistic wilderness survival courses.

14

UNDERSTANDING WILDERNESS SURVIVAL: THE VICTIM - A PROFILE

In order to complete our programme, we examined numerous courses, and questioned many instructors. It finally dawned on us that little or no research has ever been conducted on evaluating any programmes as to their effectiveness in preparing people to cope with survival situations. Following more than five years of intensive research, we eventually finalized our curricula. Working with provincial police forces, the military, and a host of Search and Rescue personnel, we examined a total of 2,029 survival occurrences.

From this data, some insights began to emerge, insights which ultimately shaped the format, content matter, and teaching methodology of our courses. With the aid of the National Association for Search and Rescue, we were able to establish a profile of the average lost victim:
- usually male (70% of all cases)
- composite outdoorsman, eg. hunter, fisherman, and camper;
- resides in urban areas;
- has the time and financial resources to spend on outdoor recreation;
- usually a novice at his activity;
- travels long distances for seasonal recreation;
- puts too much faith in material goods such as survival kits;
- travels too far and too fast to acclimatize;
- ignores signs of weather change and environmental hazards;

Snowshoes serve more than one function. Besides their obvious use,
they can be utilized as emergency shovels, windbreaks or stretchers.
The wilderness survivor must adopt a multiple-use mentality.

Discarded antlers become the source of useful tools.

- ignores body indicators in quest of predetermined goals; and
- travels from an artificial environment and does not know how to sustain life in a wilderness situation.

In addition, our police sources enabled us to effectively categorize lost victims:
1. hunters form the largest group   - 56%
2. anglers   - 24%
3. trappers   - 12%
4. hikers   - 8%

In short, of the 2,029 victims surveyed, over 1,000 were hunters; approximately 500 were fishermen; 250 were trappers; while fewer than 165 individuals were hikers.

Interestingly enough, hikers form the largest group of our students; hunters rarely participate in any of our courses.

Finally, it puzzled us as to why some victims behaved in a somewhat irrational manner. For example, some individuals:
- always move in a downward direction, even if the slope leads into a swamp;
- do not attempt to build a shelter or a fire;
- make no attempt to signal rescuers;
- run directly across roadways and back into the bush;
- hide from searchers;
- shoot at members of the search party;
- doubt their compasses or the sun's direction; and
- sleep only during mid-day due to cold and fear.

A plausible answer came from Don Johnston, Searchmaster, Lakehead Search and Rescue Unit, Thunder Bay. He believes that a victim, being frightened, could do anything. If the lost person is hysterical, he'll respond to any outside stimuli such as affection, water, a gentle voice, food, or calling out his name. Gentle persuasion will calm down this victim.

Making survival tools keeps the victim stationary, alert and occupied.

17

The lost person could easily react in another, more violent manner. If he panics, he's not thinking; hence, what the victim perceives to be happening, is happening to him. He's totally unresponsive to outside stimuli, loses all sense of control, and does not recognize such obvious features as roadways. At this stage, he'll doubt his compass or the sun's direction; furthermore, if armed, he may shoot at the rescue party.

Perhaps additional research will explain why some people react the way they do. Two questions need answering:
1. Do the circumstances precipitating a survival experience dictate a victim's type of response?
2. Can leadership style influence the group's reaction patterns?

Besides teaching survival skills, we are suggesting that competent instructors study, analyze, and delve into the mind of the wilderness victim.

SUGGESTED READING

Brown, V. Reading the Woods. New York: Collier Books, 1969.

Down But Not Out. C.F.P. 217, Ottawa: Information Canada, 1973.

Edholm, O.G. & A.L. Bacharach. The Physiology of Human Survival. Academic Press, 1965.

Elleberg, E. Hell on Ice. New York: Dodd, Mead and Co., 1938.

Fortier, E. One Survived. Anchorage: Alaska Northwest Publishing Co., 1982.

Leakey, R.E. The Making of Mankind. New York: Dutton, 1981.

Olsen, L.D. Outdoor Survival Skills. New York: Pocket Books, 1976.

Petzoldt, P. The Wilderness Handbook. New York: Norton & Co., 1974.

Read, P.P. Alive: Story of the Andes Survivors. New York: Lipincott, 1974.

Stewart, G.R. Ordeal by Hunger: The Classic Story of the Donner Party. Pocket Books, 1971.

Survival. AF Manual 64-5. Supt. of Documents, Washington, D.C.: U.S. Gov't Printing Office.

Troebst, C.C. The Art of Survival. Garden City: Doubleday, 1975.

CHAPTER 1
No one knows how much he can endure until he must.

--Richard L. Evans

AN INTRODUCTION

Only a few generations ago, the native people and the early fur trappers responded to their instincts and passed survival skills from one generation to the other. Failure to learn the skills of the forest often meant injury or death. By watching and emulating their parents, children learned the best woods to burn; how to cope with the elements; how to hunt and fish; and being reasonably comfortable in a wilderness setting. Banishment from the group or tribe often spelled certain death.

Stories of the early fur trappers abound with many survival skills mastered by these coureur-de-bois. Such skills were essential to living! The child of the wilderness could start a fire with flint and steel; read signs on the land for food, shelter, water, and danger; and finally, respect the environment which nurtured his very existence.

The outdoors were vibrant with both resources and information. Today, this information can be learned through wilderness survival courses! However, the student should be cautioned - sections of realistic wilderness survival programmes are, by their nature, harsh, brutal, and sometimes shocking. In a society that exploits the term "wilderness survival" as a selling or advertising gimmick, the student will

Although some find the bush an inhospitable and unfriendly environment, it offers the thinking survivor protection, water, food and shelter.

soon come to realize that no room exists for the philosophical arm-chair survivor in our programmes. All get their hands dirty; all experience a cold night in the bush; and all must develop a "survival mentality"!

We do not offer semi-survival or glorified camping programmes. Such courses can be dangerous, since they abstract the ugly aspects of survival: human nature under stress; snaring; the survival mentality; plant and animal procurement, preparation, consumption and use. Individuals taking part on a true survival course must be able to face, cope, and participate in activities generally not condoned by an urbanized society. Also, the participant should understand that, under realistic survival conditions, sleeping bags, matches, three changes of clothing, and a dormitory will not be on hand. Unless these concepts are faced, understood, and met, it is pointless to continue with any program called survival. Perhaps it should be labelled a wilderness experience course.

The experienced outdoorsperson remembers any messages sent out by the wilderness! To many, they emit a primordial sense of fear - fear of the bugs, hardships, and cold which presented inescapable realities to our ancestors. Perhaps this is the reason many people are terrified of the bush, lashing out at it whenever the opportunity presents itself.

If this book shows anything to the reader, it should be to work with nature and not against her. The bush is neutral; it won't help you, but it won't harm you! Fish will not jump into your pan; rabbits will not run up to you pleading to become a meal.

Careful and detailed pre-trip planning is crucial, expecially if travelling through wilderness areas. Poorly planned excursions often result in needless hardships or tragedy.

However, trees are available shelter, bedding, food, and firewood. If the student can read the signs, he'll know the upcoming weather; where the animals are congregating; and where the edible plants may be growing. To the learned person, these signs are easily understood, simple to decipher, very legible, plain, and above all, honest!

Teaching a survival course in our modern world is, at first glance, an irony. With all of our technical advance, who needs a wilderness survival program? In my opinion, we all do. Many individuals recognize the instability of our society. A power failure in New York, a middle Eastern war, a derailment in Mississauga, or a hurricane in Galveston are vivid reminders that most of the conveniences and the necessities of life arise from a house of paper cards. The malfunction of one minor part brings down the entire superstructure.

Survival skills can become a route to individual self-confidence. In our modern world, we are divorced from the process of securing shelter, water, and food - the essentials of life. Think: most of our needs are supplied to us by our government, our society, and our employer.

The more complex the world has become, the more some people desire a simple life. Even if simplicity is not possible, the urge for self-reliance remains. It is important to have a sense of self-preservation, even as the world grows more populated, more technical; and the environment, more domesticated. Also, we in the north, are almost completely surrounded by forests. A two-hour drive from downtown areas and five paces off our highways should make this impression perfectly clear. Think about it!

Finally, wilderness survival training, in our opinion, must address one's mental preparation, resourcefulness, and ability to make rational decisions under very stressful situations; it should not merely re-enforce one's camping skills.

PREVENTATIVE MEDICINE

The old adage that an ounce of prevention is worth a pound of cure can be readily applied to getting lost, and surviving, in a wilderness setting. The following list of suggestions may help prevent a potential nightmare.

If planning to take part in some backwoods activities, we advise the individual to inform a friend, family members, the region's police force, or if applicable, personnel from the Ministry of Natural Resources, as to where you are going, length of trip, and approximate time of departure. If you are not out by a predetermined period of time, ask them to send in search parties. Remember - don't forget to notify them upon your exit.

It is the opinion of many bush-wise individuals that people should not wander in the forests alone. Always travel in pairs or threes, but never by oneself. It's much too easy to break a leg, become temporarily blinded, or lose your gear. If this happens, and you're alone....????

Here is some more food for thought:

(i)   Do you carry a first aid kit, and have a working knowledge of basic first aid skills?

(ii)   What kind of condition is your vehicle in? Has it been serviced, especially before tackling those back roads?

(iii)   Do you know how to use road and topographical maps properly? Can you relate these maps to compass and aerial photographs? In reality, few are well versed in this skill.

(iv)   Are you physically and mentally ready for a trip to the backwoods?

(v)   Have you packed the proper gear, such as waterproof matches (strike anywhere) in an air tight container? Has all lightweight food been placed in a grub bag, (so it can hang in a tree, not in the tent)?

(vi)   Has all clothing (as well as sleeping bag) been wrapped in waterproof plastic containers?

(vii)   Do you know what your gear is meant to - and not meant to do? Has it been abused?

(viii) Are you carrying strike-anywhere, waterproof matches? Do you have a secondary fire-starting source?

(ix)   Is survival gear safely stored on your person?

You should consider the implications of these questions and comments, realizing the potential hazards which may occur if your replies point to carelessness, inexperience, and just plain lack of common sense.

ON YOUR PERSON

Despite these safety precautions, some people may nonetheless wind up in a desperate survival situation. If this is the case, we strongly advise the victim to:

Empty all pockets. Do you have dry matches, a knife or extra food? Use your ingenuity to see how you can use what is available to you. Depending on the circumstances, we recommend a systematic and rational approach to coping with the wilds. First, constructing a shelter is extremely important; a warm. dry, comfortable shelter is mandatory. During the winter, one cannot survive long in bad weather without one. Water is next - locating a source of fresh water is extremely important. A fast flowing stream is not necessarily safe if a carcass is rotting upstream. Although food is necessary, people have lasted several weeks without it. When collecting food, know what you are collecting - don't guess - poisonous plants can look like an edible variety. When foraging, keep in mind that more calorie intake must be harvested than expended; similarly, for your fire (which provides a psychological value, as well as warmth) begin to collect firewood as far away from your shelter as feasible. As your energy decreases with time, harvest closer; hence you will not need to travel far to get firewood.

Once established at a site preferably near a vehicle (car or plane), build a signal to attract the attention of your rescuers. These include three signal fires (with thick, dense smoke), or three logs tied together in the shape of a triangle, or, in a real bind, set ablaze a peeling, solitary birch tree. You may survive the wilderness, and this act may attract some urban antagonists but "...better to be judged by twelve than carried by six." Live to apologize later. We advise the victim to remain by his shelter, relax, and drink copious amounts of liquid.

Incidentally, the most destructive attitude prevalent among many Canadians is the "It can't happen to me" attitude; and yet, an average of 600 individuals are lost yearly in Ontario alone! As well, many picture the forest as a romantic place, alive with animals and plants; however, the truth of the matter is that while the beauty is present, so are the bugs, poisonous plants, and an hostile environment. The bush is entirely neutral! Although it won't harm you, the forest will not offer assistance to those ignorant of its ways and characteristics. A tutored victim on the other hand, will be able to "read" the wilderness and know how to construct shelters utilizing local materials; which plants are edible; and where to set up snares and deadfalls.

Above all, sit down, relax, and admit you're lost. Once this realization becomes clear, make the best of any given predicament. Research supports our belief that wilderness survival is mostly dependent on the victim's will to live! In our opinion, more than 80% of surviving a wilderness emergency depends on a disciplined, positive mental attitude; 20% or less relies on bush skills.

A calm individual is more likely to think clearly, and follow a common-sense approach to survival. Panic, on the other hand, is infectious and has killed more people (even those lost with full packs on their backs) than any other single factor. Remember to stop, take stock of the situation, and admit to yourself that you're lost.

As difficult as the situation may be, it is important to maintain a positive outlook; you will be found! The will to live is a reality that usually makes the difference between finding you alive...or dead.

TRAVELLING - A SURVIVAL SITUATION

Quite often, the debate between travelling or remaining stationary comes up. When to travel and when to stay put is not an easy decision. You've got to know when the decision to travel is a good one, since the results of a poorly planned decision to move could prove fatal.

Let's discuss when to move and when not to move: the victim should be able to make an intelligent decision concerning travel in a survival situation.

Travel in a cold weather environment is extremely difficult and hazardous. The decision to travel should be reached only after careful consideration of the following requirements for successful travel:

- (1) Exact knowledge of your present location and the objective of the journey.
- (2) Knowledge of orientation methods.
- (3) Unusual amount of physical stamina.
- (4) Suitable clothing.
- (5) Adequate food, fuel, and shelter or the equipment for obtaining them.
- (6) Additional considerations:
  - (a) Your chances of being located by a search party are greater if you stay with your vehicle.
  - (b) It takes twice as much food (energy) to travel as it does to wait for pick-up.
  - (c) There may not be adequate shelter along your proposed route of travel.

Therefore, stay put unless it is dangerous or impractical.

If you do decide to travel, leave a note at the vehicle site and some signal indicating the direction you went. Choose to travel only after a careful consideration of the many variables.

DIRECTION FINDING WITHOUT A COMPASS

Survival victims are occasionally faced with one agonizing decision: should they move or remain stationary. We normally advise the latter; however, there may be circumstantial, geographic, or other factors which could necessitate the abandonment of one's original site. These reasons include a lack of food, water, or wood supply; hazards, such as snow or rock slides; the danger of flooding; inadequate protection from the elements; insufficient materials for proper shelter construction; and poor signalling opportunities to attract search parties.

Only when these (or any other unforeseen) problems exist do we advise the victim to abandon his site. In addition, before making such a move, we suggest that the survivor leave behind a note outlining where (and when) he went. In the event that rescuers do find the original site, they'll know the survivor's new location. Furthermore, the victim should <u>blaze</u> his way, thus facilitating his being found.

Sometimes the move in question is quite close - over the next hill, downriver a short distance, or into the next valley. However, circumstances may dictate travelling much farther. If this is the case, a survivor must be capable of "reading" the wilderness in order to navigate through bushlands, especially if a compass is not available.

The following techniques have been tried and tested in wilderness areas throughout much of Canada. With practice, the victim will be quite capable of direction finding...without a compass.

The Big Dipper

The Big Dipper is one of the best known star formations; it is bright, and fairly unique. Using the two stars at the end of the pan, look for the North Star which will be about four times the distance away as the distance between these two stars. Although the Big Dipper rotates, these two stars will always point towards Polaris because the Dipper rotates around it. Face Polaris and you will be facing North.

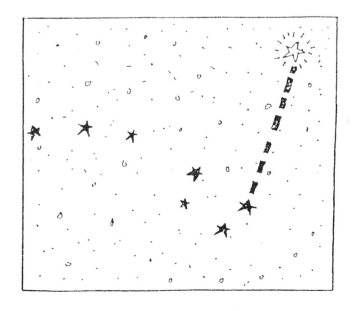

Watch Method

Hold a watch flat in your hand. Turn the watch until the hour hand points directly at the sun. Between the hours of 6 a.m. and 6 p.m. (standard time) a line from the center of the watch, dividing the small angle between the hour hand and 12 o'clock will point SOUTH.

Some people cannot perceive using a digital watch; however, a rational person can draw the hour and minute hands on paper or if need be, on the ground. In so doing, (s)he can now locate north using this method.

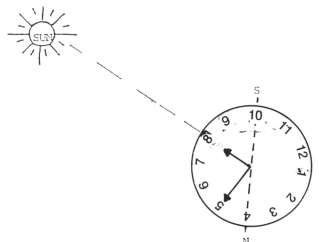

Shadow Stick

A third method of finding north is to place a long stick in the ground, and as the sun progresses, mark the end of the shadow at intervals of fifteen minutes or more. Draw a straight line (A) along the line marks and this will indicate east and west. North will therefore be at the right angle to this line.

As simple as this method may sound, many individuals have a great deal of difficulty understanding the principle behind this technique. This illustrated description may be of some help.

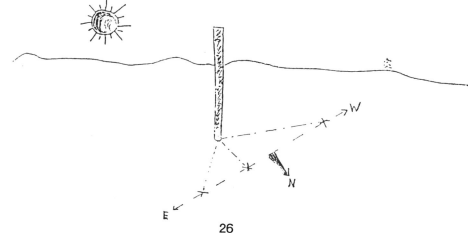

26

STEP ONE:
Find an open stretch of ground where the sun's rays fall unobstructed. Place twig 1 into ground. Place twig 2 at end of first twig's shadow.

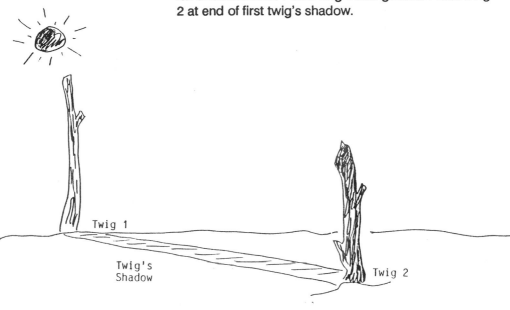

Twig 1

Twig's Shadow

Twig 2

STEP TWO:
After one hour, place third twig at new shadow's end. The longer the survivor waits to place twig 3, the more accurate the final reading.

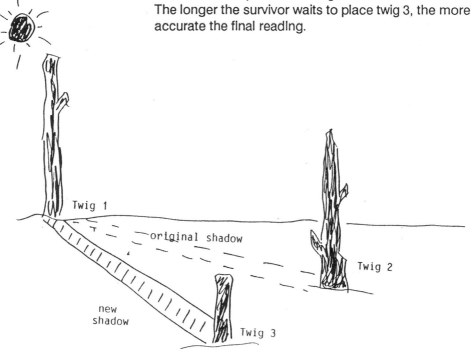

Twig 1

original shadow

Twig 2

new shadow

Twig 3

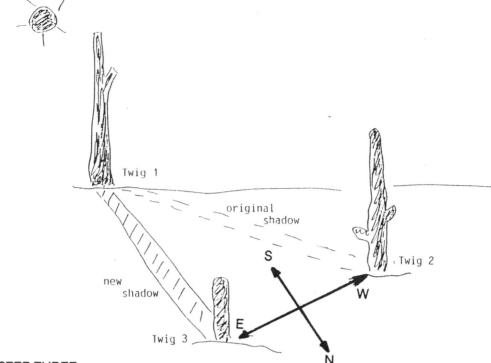

STEP THREE:

Draw a line from twig 2 to twig 3. This is an East-West line.

Draw another line perpendicular to the East - West line. This is your North - South line.

As previously mentioned, the longer the survivor waits before placing twig 3, the more accurate his readings will be, since the angle of the two shadows will be more pronounced.

Utilizing the Sun

An obvious method of direction finding is using the sun itself. During the spring, summer, and fall, it rises in the east and sets in the west. During the winter months, however, the sun rises more in a south-easterly direction and sets in the south-west.

White Pines

In our region of North America, the prevailing winds blow from the north-west. The constantly blowing winds tend to bend tall, mature trees (especially White Pines) towards the southeast. When analyzing their growth patterns, the survivor will note that not only do the tops point in a south-easterly direction, but that the entire top half of White Pines also grow towards the south-east.

An individual attempting to utilize this method of direction finding does not rely solely on a few trees. Instead, he chooses a large sample, then averages his approximation of south-east.

The Forest Itself

In level zones where the dense bush meets an open area such as field or lakes, the northern side of the forest, especially the undergrowth, will have a netted, or "set" appearance. Although difficult to initially detect, the trained observer can usually notice this "matting" effect.

Incidentally, in exposed areas, a tree's bark is generally thicker, and the rings in the timber are closer together in the north side. Also, little or no branching takes place on the exposed north side; most growth is on the tree's southern flank.

Southern Exposures

During the winter months, especially in February and March, there will be more snow accumulation on the northern slopes. Southern exposures may contain little or no snow.

Other Techniques

Two other methods of direction findings that have been reported to me by a number of bush-wise individuals include:
  i) Flying Squirrel Holes - apparently these face south.
  ii) Pileated Woodpeckers - these birds dig their homes on the east side of a
     tree.

Although, any one of these direction finding techniques may prove futile or inaccurate, when the survivor looks at the total picture, that is, observes the relationship between all of these methods and averages a general direction of travel, the combination of all these techniques will prove to be amazingly accurate.

TRAIL BLAZING

Although the survivor is advised not to wander too far from his vehicle or shelter, unforseen circumstances may force the victim to seek a more suitable location. If he knows the approximate direction to another site, these techniques will offer some assistance. However, in the event that a search party locates the old site, a note outlining the direction of travel should be left behind in the vehicle or shelter.

It is advisable to thoroughly trail blaze the entire route. This greatly facilitates the efforts of a search party. It is also the survivor's safety line: should he lose his way, he can retrace his trail.

SOME TRAIL BLAZING SYMBOLS

CONTINUE STRAIGHT AHEAD

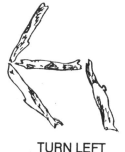

TURN LEFT

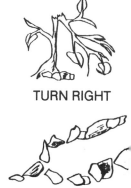

TURN RIGHT

TURN RIGHT

TURN LEFT

SOME EMERGENCY SIGNALS

The most important member of a rescue unit may very well be the survivor himself. His knowledge and ability to do his part in the efforts to locate and return him to civilization is quite often critical and may make the difference between the success or failure of a search and rescue mission. In many cases, the survivor has been the only untrained, unequipped, and unprepared element that constitutes the overall Search and Rescue complex. Such have often proven fatal!

As I write these words, the sad story of one victim comes to mind. Several years ago, an inexperienced camper decided to backpack into the boreal forests of central Alaska. He was spotted by a bush pilot. Although, as the victim's journal later points out, the camper was experiencing extreme hardships, he mistakingly gave the "All Well" signal to the plane, a mistake which cost him his life! His emaciated body was found some months later.

It is a proven fact that the well trained, equipped, and prepared survivor has a much better chance of seeing mom and the kids again. One simply must know what to do in a survival situation to assist the search party.

The survivor must be able to use effective signals to communicate with his rescuers. This includes ground to air signals, day and night signal flares, signal mirrors, and any other type of signalling device, including whistles and rifles.

There are many ways to construct ground to air signals. For example, keeping aircraft wreckage clear of fresh snow provides contrast and reflection of sun/moonlight, thereby making the aircraft/car a signal in itself.

Use natural materials such as boughs, small trees, and sod to attract the searcher's attention.

Sod can be turned over to provide contrast with the existing background while boughs and trees are normally laid out to form any type of ground to air signals (see list). When constructing these signals, they must be constructed as large as possible, without running into the edge of trees or shadows. Also, they should be placed in areas that provide the greatest amount of visibility from the air. Concerning shape, construct signals in such a way as to provide angularity and contrast. Sharp, clear-cut lines and angles will usually denote man-made structures and not those formed by nature. Finally, maintain your signals by removing fallen snow and by constant additions in order to improve contrast.

With regard to signal fires, they should be large enough to enable heat to carry smoke straight up and through any inversion layer. Throughout the day, attempt to signal aircraft that may, without your knowledge, be off on the horizon. Flame-producing materials such as tinder and kindling should be gathered and kept in readiness in large quantities. Application of such materials to the already burning fire will produce an almost immediate and intense flame, while smoke-producing materials are also kept in readiness and in large quantities. Boughs are one of the best smoke-producing materials. They partially smother a fire, and, when allowed burn, produce a grey-colored smoke. Birch bark added to a fire will produce black smoke and adds contrast.

Built off the ground and covered with boughs, this fire signal burns very rapidly. Fanned by an incoming supply of oxygen, flames force the resulting blanket of smoke high into the air. The thick covering of boughs also help to keep tinder dry at all times. This same effect could be created by piling a supply of timber and kindling under a solitary coniferous tree.

My favourite type of signal fire is the elevated tripod. This is easily and quickly constructed by lashing three untrimmed saplings together to form a tripod; halfway up the tripod, build a rack. On this rack, place plenty of birch bark and lots of kindling. Cover the entire structure with boughs.

In order to light, reach <u>underneath</u> the tripod; a small flame, when coming in contact with the bark, will produce a blazing inferno!

Built off the ground with boughs, this fire signal burns very rapidly. Fanned by an incoming supply of oxygen, flames force the resulting blanket of smoke high into the air. The thick covering of boughs also helps to keep the tinder dry at all times.

In areas where saplings are unavailable, this same effect could be created by piling a supply of tinder and kindling under a solitary conifer; ideally, this should be a medium-sized tree situated in a clearing.

If caught away from all previously prepared signals, set ablaze an individual birch tree, preferably one covered with loose, papery bark. The resulting smoke is dark, thick, and will be seen from great distances.

Should potassium permanganate be available in your first aid kit, a handful of this chemical thrown on wet snow will produce an instant distress signal: a large, bright, purple blotch of stained snow, clearly visible from the air.

Signal mirrors are found in just about all survival kits. These simple devices are credited with contributing to numerous rescues. Simply angle a mirror or shining metallic object to attract a plane's attention.

When a gun or whistle is available, <u>three</u> shots (or whistle blasts), fired at regular intervals, will attract the attention of a nearby search and rescue team. Any signals grouped in three - three fires, three piles of rocks or three shots - are international distress signals.

You are urged to understand and master these signals, since, quite conceivably they could save your life!

SOME EMERGENCY SIGNALS

KEY   CODE

1.   Require Doctor, Serious injuries   ▬ ▬

2.   Require Medical Supplies   ═

3.   Unable to Proceed   X

4.   Require Food and Water   F

5.   Am Proceeding in this Direction   →

6.   Probably Safe to Land Here   △

7.   All Well   L LL

8.   Require Assistance
      (3 fires in a triangle)

Comfort is not essential to survival, and is often valued too highly. You must value your life more than comfort and be willing to tolerate heat, cold, hunger, dirt, itching, pain, and almost any discomfort. If you expose yourself to self-pity because you have a blister and think you cannot go any further, you have not thought the situation over. Whatever comes, this too shall pass away.

E. W. Wilcox

SURVIVAL SHELTERS

Individuals taking part in almost any extended outdoor activity should be capable of building and maintaining a survival shelter. It is not a difficult skill to learn, yet this knowledge could mean the difference between life and death. The type of shelter that one chooses to construct will vary depending upon his particular skills, the season, materials at hand, and the type of terrain in which the survivor finds himself.

The location of any shelter is as important as the shelter itself. The survivor should consider the following criteria:

(i)   Are materials for shelter construction and fuel for fires readily available?
(ii)   Is a water source nearby? Any signs of food?
(iii)   Have you evaluated dangers such as floods, avalanches, or wild animals?
(iv)   Is the area easily seen by search and rescue parties? Can a signal system by set up?
(v)   Location will vary according to season. Spring and summer sites should be in clear, breezy places, as reprise from bugs. During the fall and winter, seek sheltered areas, away from low-lying cold sinks, preferably in a south-facing slope, half way up the hill.

Prior to constructing any large scale duplex, the survivor is well advised to search carefully for any existing natural shelters. These include large, hollow trees, a blown over rooting system, caves, or overhanging rock outcrops. Such features can at least form the foundation on which to build a snug shelter.

Our suggestion is to make a small, easily constructed, cozy shelter. There are occasions, however, when the building of a semi-permanent type of dwelling may be necessary. This is true if the survivor has all the necessary materials and manpower, and is faced with the possibility of an extended stay in the wilderness.

CANOE SHELTER

Prop the canoe on a 45 degree angle. Use a Y-shaped support sapling to hold up the canoe, while a tree, rock, or any permanent object acts as a brace. Lean additional "ribs" on the exposed side, later covering entire side with boughs, plastic, or poncho. Add mud or rocks at top and bottom of poncho to keep covering in place. To keep from billowing, add branches, sapling, or any available poles over the plastic.

Once sleeping area has been insulated with a minimum of 30 cm of boughs, this shelter is snug, completely water-proof, and easily capable of sheltering two people.

For maximum protection from the elements, face the exposed (side covered with poncho) away from the prevailing winds.

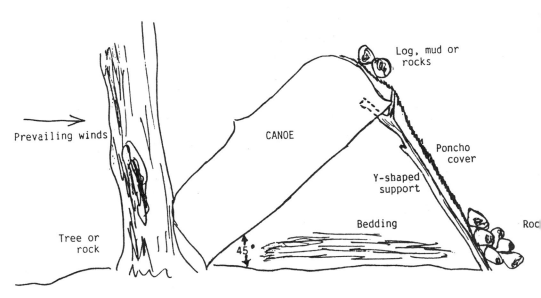

THE SIMPLE A-FRAME SHELTER

Wedge a 2.5 metre (approximately) sapling between two Y-shaped supports. Place appropriate "ribs" onto the main ridgepole. Cover the entire structure with plastic, raincoat, or boughs. If a tarp is available, leave enough covering at the entrance way to allow for flaps, which can be folded over to completely cover the entrance. Pile stones, logs, or mud at the base to hold down the covering. A layer of leaves, branches, and boughs added on top of the poncho offers extra protection from the elements. This shelter is totally free-standing; no string or lashing of any kind is required. The angle or pitch of the roof should be no less than 45 degrees. In the event of torrential rains, this steep roof sheds water quite effectively.

Insulate sleeping area with at least 30 cm of boughs.

The entrance to this shelter should face away from the prevailing winds.

Inter-woven rib structure of the simple A-frame shelter. Lashing of any kind is not required.

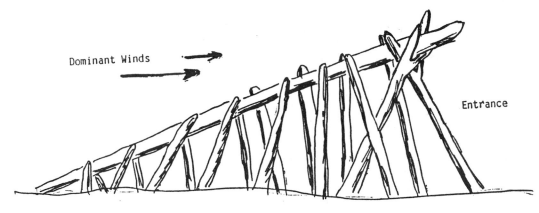

Dominant Winds

Entrance

THE LEAN-TO

The term lean-to covers many different types of survival shelters.

Generally, there is a pole framework covered with a wide array of materials; sometimes, it is more advantageous to utilize a few trees found two or three metres apart, assuming that the location, water, firewood and other needs are in the immediate vicinity. Level and firm ground is advantageous. Approximately one metre off the ground, run a branch horizontally from one tree to the other, then run other branches from this sapling down to the ground at approximately a 45 degree angle. The height of your horizontal pole, and the distance between the two large trees is the size of the opening you will be left with. Variations are possible but it is best to try and make this opening the correct size from the beginning. A tripod may be used instead of tall heavy trees. Always remember that heat rises; also, the higher the roof, the more efficient it will shed rain. However, an exceptionally steep roof seriously cuts down on interior space. A 45 degree angle is thought by many people to be a good compromise. After completing the framework, look for a good covering. Spruce boughs make an excellent natural covering and will do in a survival situation. If available, a sheet of plastic does an excellent job. When using bark or boughs place them at the bottom of the roof and work your way up. This way of overlapping is similar to the way in which shingles are laid on a roof; if worried about a cold night, choose a site where the opening of your lean-to will face a large rock. Build a fire against this rock. This will reflect heat from the fire back into your shelter. A mistake many people make with lean-to's is choosing a low depression area in which to build. Shortly after the commencement of a rainstorm, the lean-to turns into a covered swimming pool.

SEMI-PERMANENT SHELTERS

A variety of shelters, designed to be somewhat more permanent than the lean-to can be built given a longer time span. Most shelters of this type are best erected when some man-made fabrics and materials are available. The teepee is a good example.

Cut three poles approximately four metres in length and tie together at the 3.5 metre mark. Use these to set up a tripod, then continue placing extra poles about the tripod until a semi-enclosed circular dwelling is made. You have several choices at his point. If you continue to place more poles, the dwelling becomes reasonably secure and waterproof. In a rainstorm, most of the water will drip down the poles, leaving the centre of the dwelling dry. On the other hand, one could use bark to build up your walls on the outside of the poles. The best alternative is to use a fabric of some sort, such as a tarpaulin, blankets, parachute, or sheets of plastic. Remember: during all this building, leave an entrance way facing away from the prevailing winds.

The tarp cabin is simply a different version of the teepee. Four walls are built, as in log cabin construction, to a height of about one metre. Now using a framework of poles form the corners to complete the roof in teepee fashion. With any shelter, a thick roof is preferable since it will give better insulation and water shedding success. A small fire can be built near a mud-packed corner. Be sure to leave a small hole for ventilation.

LOG SHELTER

This is another example of a semi-permanent type of shelter. It is built against a large, flat rock at least two metres high and three metres in length.

A considerable amount of trees are needed, since the logs are placed side by side forming a very tight, secure, wind and water-proof roof.

If cutting live trees, it is wise to make use of softwoods in the construction as it will make the work easier, as well as saving yourself some energy. Otherwise, scrounge for dead timber. All trees are trimmed of limbs and laid side by side against the rock at a 45 degree angle; chink the gaps between the logs with moss, mud, and leaves. Place a layer of deciduous leaves and coniferous boughs over the mud, since it is this final layer that will keep out most of the heavy rains. This final layer is also an excellent insulator.

To finish off the two side openings, weave small branches to form walls, covering them with several layers of boughs, or if available, a ground sheet. Inside the shelter, place at least 30 cm of evergreen boughs on the floor. This provides comfort, insulation from the cold ground, and should rain seep inside, the bedding keeps the survivor from wallowing in the dampness. Keep the doorway small.

Due to its size and shape, a small fireplace can be built in a corner against the rock face. Place a sufficient quantity of stones around it to block any flying sparks, since green boughs burn very rapidly. Also, make a small hole in the roof above the fireplace, thereby allowing smoke to escape.

The log shelter is quite dark inside. From the interior, the small doorway acts as a source of light. Since most insects are attracted to light, they tend to simply fly out the door. A small punky fire will also help to repel insects.

When constructing these shelters, the survivor must remember that they are designed to protect him from the elements; they are not meant to replace one's posh living room! If uncomfortable, so be it! Comfort is not essential to survival and in some cases, is valued too highly. The victim must regard living more than comfort, and be willing to tolerate heat, cold, itching, bugs, pain, and almost any form of discomfort. If the survivor exposes himself to self-pity beacuse of a few drops of water dripping on his head or some mosquito bites, and believes he can't go on living, he has not thought the situation over.

This is one aspect of survival that students must learn and master.

SNOW SHELTERS: THE QUINZHEE

A snow shelter is known by many names: snow house, snow hut, or quinzhee. All, however, stand for the same thing: a hollow mound of snow which the victim shapes in order to spend one or more nights inside. The principle behind this shelter is to take advantage of the insulating air pockets trapped between fluffy snow; it also keeps the victim out of direct winds.

Chink all roof openings. Log shelters require a great deal of time and patience to erect. They are, however, warm, comfortable and waterproof.

By using a shovel, snowshoes, pots, or even hands, one can make this type of shelter. But be forewarned - it takes several hours of wet, back-breaking work to create a good shelter. No doubt, the victim may become wet from both perspiration and melting snow. We advise the individual to choose a site which provides snow, protection from the wind, boughs for your bedding, and an area free from tree stumps and logs.

Begin with piling snow 2-3 metres high and 3 metres in diameter. Let stand for a few hours to settle and crystallize; some people prefer to gently tramp down on the snow with snowshoes to speed up this process. Tunnel into the snow and move upwards towards the centre of the ceiling. It is important to keep the roof to a thickness of 20 to 30 centimeters or risk the dangers of a cave-in. To check for the proper thickness, periodically poke through the walls with a stick.

As you scrape away snow, leave a large flat area for a sleeping shelf. The shelf should easily accommodate everyone planning to occupy the shelter. To take advantage of the higher, warmer air (trapped at the roof) build the sleeping area fairly high; the

Complete winter shelter. Entire structure, especially sleeping platform, is higher than surrounding area.

top of the sleeping shelf should not be lower than the top of the entrance. To provide ventilation, poke a hole on the side of the roof. This is especially important if a small fire, candle, or lamp is kept burning inside. Great care must be taken when raising the temperature of the shelter. Dripping water from the ceiling will result in wet clothing and sleeping gear. Eventually, the roof will collapse. Try not to raise the temperature so high that the shelter melts around you. Occasionally add more snow onto the roof. This is extra insulation. To provide suitable bedding and insulation material, a (minimum) 30 cm layer of boughs must be laid on the shelf. Some boughs should also cover the floor and entrance way. Sleeping directly on snow only works in fiction, even with the best sleeping bag. Finally, a pile of snow or snowshoes should be placed at the entrance to block the wind and keep the heat from escaping out of the shelter. It is also advisable to erect a snow (or tree) wall near the entrance way to prevent any winds from funneling into the shelter.

SNOW CAVE

Snowcaves are usually built on the windward side of a hill, where snow banks or drifts form due to the direction and activity of the wind. Begin by measuring the thickness of a drift with a slender 2 to 4 metre long sapling. Feel the snow to estimate the degree of its compaction to see if further packing is necessary.

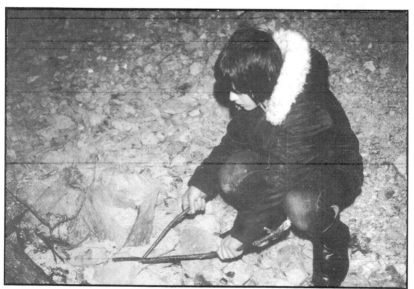

Small, heated stones, when placed by cold feet, offer warmth during most of the night.

Use any available saplings for roofing beams. Cover entirely with boughs and snow, leaving small opening over fireplace.

The cave itself is built two thirds of the way up the hill, above the frost pocket. It should not be made near the bottom of the hill, since this is usually the coldest spot (cold air settles, warm air rises).

Constructing the cave involves the slow process of digging out snow with any available tool, including snowshoes, pots, or hands. Individuals involved in this activity can count on getting wet, cold, and exhausted. Occasionally, a twig is used to check the thickness of the walls (approximately 20 - 30 cm). The sleeping platform should be higher than the entrance tunnel. A small hole near the roof serves to ventilate the cave. When digging, tunnel upwards, then inwards to minimize the danger of a cave-in. Since little or no piling of snow is required to construct this shelter, snow caves are usually easier to build than the quinzhee.

Snow shelters are very effective survival devices only if suitable sleeping gear is available; otherwise, the victim faces a cold, long, and miserable night. Nonetheless, inside the mound of snow, the victim will be considerably warmer than if he were outside. Regardless of how cold it is outside, the temperature inside the shelter will not dip too much below the freezing point. Although a howling blizzard is blowing on the exterior, little noise will be heard inside. The more snow is piled on top of this shelter, the more insulated and soundproof it becomes.

SNOW CAVE

No piling of snow is required when constructing a snow cave.
Compress snowbank or drift as much as possible, and tunnel up, and in. (same as snow shelter)
Do so slowly, checking for proper thickness of walls (approximately 20-30 cm).
Sleeping platform should be higher than the entrance way.

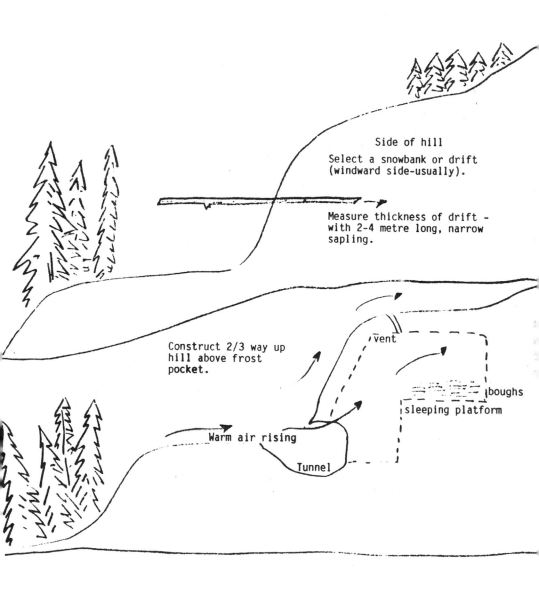

Side of hill

Select a snowbank or drift (windward side-usually).

Measure thickness of drift - with 2-4 metre long, narrow sapling.

Construct 2/3 way up hill above frost pocket.

Vent

boughs

sleeping platform

Warm air rising

Tunnel

Use supply of firewood as windbreak. Always harvest more wood than is needed. Should a storm strike suddenly, there is no need to leave shelter.

HEATED WINTER SHELTERS

Locate a slightly slanted area with a rock the length of one's body and approximately one metre high. Scrape away all snow from the desired length and width of the sleeping area. Place this excess snow at the sides and end of the shelter. This will be used later to cover roof and sides. Two Y-shaped supports, firmly embedded in snow, hold up a crossbeam paralleling the rock. Add saplings from this beam to the rock. Other poles can be placed at side and end, leaving front open. Boughs are added onto this framework. Place a layer of snow on boughs, but not directly over fire area. Layer entire sleeping area with 20 cm of boughs, keeping all branches away from fireplace.

The required firewood, broken into manageable pieces, is stacked in the entrance way, providing an effective windbreak. Incidentally, always harvest more firewood than is needed. In the event of a storm, you won't need to venture out of your shelter.

The lowest part of shelter should house fireplace, while highest area is the sleeping zone. We have slept comfortably in this shelter without any blankets or sleeping bags during the coldest part of the winter months. For additional windbreak protection, add some small conifers near the entrance.

44

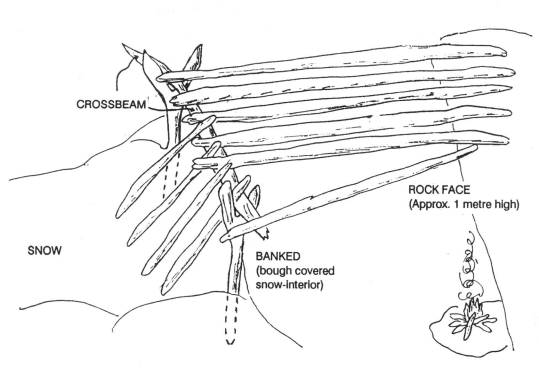

CROSSBEAM

ROCK FACE
(Approx. 1 metre high)

SNOW

BANKED
(bough covered
snow-interior)

THE STONE SHELTER

As every one knows, all survival texts, including the one we've written, have an extensive section dealing with the lean-to. However, I hope that thinking individuals realize that any shelter, including the lean-to, has its limitations. Lean-to's are fine in the spring, summer, and early fall. But during late fall and winter....forget it! If a sleeping bag is available, any type of poorly constructed shelter will suffice. But if no covers of any kind are on hand, the entire scenario changes drastically. Keep a fire going all night, you say? That might be one solution.

It would be ideal to stack all of the required wood in one pile, set it on fire, and relax for a ten-hour sleep. But this is sheer lunacy!

Let's face reality and try to visualize how a lean-to might work under cold, harsh conditions. You throw some fair sized logs on the fire. As they burn, you feel a warming glow. Suddenly, one side is too warm, so you roll over to heat the other side, or try to move a little further away from the fire. This process continues until the fire burns lower and chilling begins - a cycle rarely lasting more than an hour.

So you get up and start all over again. Too hot, then too cold! However, if a system could be devised to store the excess heat and have it released slowly while you sleep comfortably, all our problems would be solved.

Recently, I took a trip to the small community of Emsdale, a sleepy village nestled somewhere between Huntsville and North Bay. A friend had to pick up some cedar logs and invited me to come along. The road, icy and slippery, took us deep into the backwoods, where an aged woodcutter lived with his wife, without the benefit of a telephone, electricity, or running water. His house was heated by a wood-burning stove, situated in the middle of his basement. Interestingly enough, the stove was completely surrounded by layered stones, piled one metre high. Why? I asked. The reply: all day long the rocks get heated. At night, they slowly release their heat, enough heat to warm up the entire house until daylight.

Indeed, during the winter months, when a lean-to is next to useless, rocks are a man's best friend. Heat a rock for a number of hours and you will be pleasantly surprised at how long it will give off heat. Although not always available in every situation, any wilderness areas contain a fair amount of exposed bedrock. Time spent looking for the right rock is time well spent in terms of comfort.

Ideally, the right rock should be two to three metres long, and flat on the sleeping side. Let's call this the main heat wall. This must be approximately one metre high and perpendicular, or, better still, gently sloping inwardly towards its base. This is good, but what is even better is to have a similar rock paralleling the main heat wall, about one metre distance. In essence, you would have two heat walls. If small, movable rocks are around, pry them out of the frozen ground with logs, and using leverage place them at one end of the main heat walls to form a three-sided rock

"Burning" the main wall. During the night, hot rocks will release heat.
Depending on their size and shape, stones release two to three hours
of heat for every hour they're burned.

shelter. These last two walls, however, are a luxury and not a complete necessity. However, in severe weather, two parallel walls are needed even if one of these walls has to be constructed using the smaller, movable rocks.

To heat the rocks, remove all of the snow between the walls and start fires close to each wall. Once these fires are going, continue to feed them larger pieces of wood, i.e. whole, manageable, dead softwood trees. Allow the huge flames to scorch the rocks for at least three hours.

Remember, remove <u>all</u> snow from the tops of the main heating walls, or the resulting melted waters will cool off the rocks.

Some rocks have a better capacity to absorb heat than others. Stay away from ice covered rocks. This could be a sign that on warmer days, water dripped over the flat surface that you're trying to heat. It stands to reason that such a rock will have absorbed a fair amount of moisture and will probably break off in flat chunks as it heats up. Result: very little heat absorbed, and a lesser amount radiated during the night.

The longer the walls are heated, the longer they will give off heat. While the fires are burning, you gather more logs, collect boughs for roofing and bedding, saplings, and dry out wet clothing. Ideal rocks can give off heat for up to three times as long as the amount of time they were heated.

Once the walls have been thoroughly heated, allow fire to die out. When it is completely dead, remove the remaining live coals with a stick. Take care that no live coals are left.

Next step: Utilizing the same stick, place at least five centimeters of soil (located under the coals) over the ashes. On this soil, place a thin layer of bedding; if boughs are laid down, they should be covered with a poncho, or steaming will occur during the night. Otherwise, one could sleep directly on the warm soil.

Now quickly throw on the roof. Naturally, all materials were collected during daylight hours. Using straight limbs for framework, lay these poles over the walls, layering a thick blanket of evergreen boughs over these poles. A small conifer tree could act as a doorway to the shelter. Your stone shelter is now completed. Crawl in and have a good, comfortable, and warm sleep!

Experience has taught me that the timing for the final stages of constructing this type of shelter is crucial. No more than twenty minutes should elapse from the charcoal removing stage to the completed product. Lingering past this twenty minute deadline causes the walls to lose too much of their heat. I strongly advise the survivalist to work well into the winter night, starting to burn his shelter at approximately 4:30 p.m. Fire is put out by 8:30 p.m., thereby, ensuring a full night's sleep. Again, all materials should be gathered during daylight hours.

Another hint: chink all holes in the constructed walls with boughs, thereby preventing any winds from howling into your shelter. Once all this work has been done, you are ready to relax. Crawl in head first, and remove a lot of your heavy clothing. You will be comfortable for a couple of hours. As you become cold, put these clothes back on. Under no circumstances must you sweat, or chilling will result.

But what happens if stranded in an area without rocks? Don't despair.

Locate a sheltered area, clearing away snow from the desired sleeping area. Build fires on top of this area, with the same intensity and technique used in the heating of stone shelters. After a few hours, remove the live coals, and cover the ashes with soil. An inverted A-frame shelter (see diagram) is built over this heated ground. Again, experience has taught me two things:
(1) Time is of the essence. Again, a twenty minute deadline is crucial.
(2) Collect all materials during daylight hours or groping at night for boughs will produce negative results.

Sleeping out in winter without benefit of tents or sleeping bags is a most gratifying experience. What a feeling! No longer an armchair survival expert! Experiment until your techniques regarding survival shelters are best suited to you, even if such experiences are time consuming, demanding, and emotionally expensive.

Sleeping area between main heat wall and stone sides.

Birch bark conical shelter built overlooking a large lake. This open site provides some welcome relief from bugs, makes the victim more visible to searchers, and keeps the survivor well supplied with water. In our northern regions, water in most rivers, lakes, streams, and bogs is fit to drink. Prior to drinking, always check surrounding waters for contaminants such as animal droppings or carcasses.

Utilizing his mental resources, the survivor can combine the desired characteristics of all these shelters to construct one which best suits his primary needs. For example, summer shelters should be relatively high and sloping. This allows for an interior smudge fire and the rapid shedding of rainfall. During the winter, the survivor's shelter needs to be much smaller and covered with snow to entrap any precious heat, and built in protected areas but not at the bottom of a valley.

Our advice is to experiment with several varieties, and finally, settle with a model best suiting the individual, the circumstances, and the season. One should then practice building the desired shelter(s) until they become second nature.

It is expected of the athlete, sportsman, camper, or marksman to practice his skills. Why should this philosophy not apply to the neophyte wishing to master any number of wilderness survival skills?

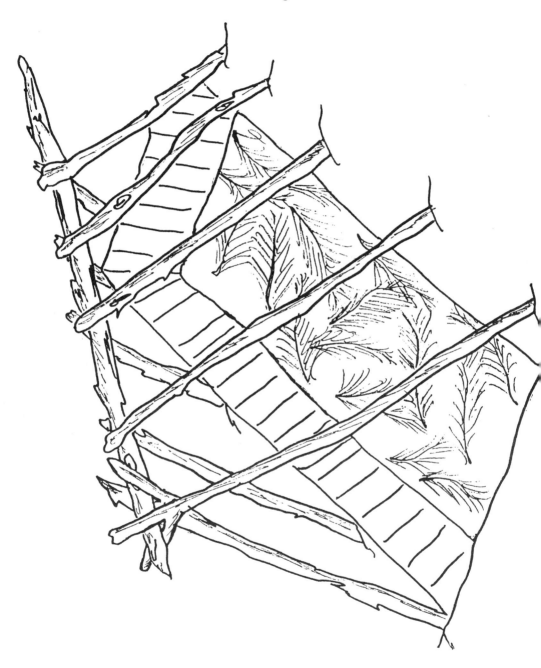

A-frame shelter covering a heated section of ground.

´ If possible, the survivor should utilize natural shelters, such as rock overhangs, caves, or tree roots.

SUGGESTED READING

Angier, B. *How to Stay Alive in the Woods*. New York: Collier Books, 1974.

Auel, J.M. *The Valley of the Horses*. Toronto: Bantam Books, 1982.

Brown, T. and Hunter, R. *Concise Book of Survival and Rescue.* Agincourt: Gage, 1978.

Colby, C.B., Angier, B. *The Art & Science of Taking to the Woods.* New York: Collier, 1971.

Ferrl, G. "Signals Can Save Your Life." *Angler and Hunter*, March, 1987, p. 50.

Ferri, G. "Preparing for the Trip." *Angler and Hunter*, March, 1986, p. 47.

Heyl, F. *Staying Alive in the Arctic.* Lake Oswego: Plant Deck, Inc.

Northern Survival. R 72-5172, Ottawa: Information Canada, 1976.

Kjellstrom, B. *Be Expert With Map and Compass*. New York: Charles Scribner and Sons, 1975.

Reed, W.M. *Patterns in the Sky*. New York: Morrow and Company, 1951.

Risk, P.H. *Outdoor Safety and Survival*. New York: John Wiley and Sons, 1983.

Rutstrum, C. *The Wilderness Route Finde*r. New York: Collier Books, 1973.

Spotters Guide. CFP 147, Ottawa: Information Canada, 1975.

Stefansson, V. *Arctic Manual.* New York: MacMillan and Co., 1944.

Survival Manual. Denver, Colo.: Colorado Dept. of Natural Resources.

Whelan, T. and B. Angier. *On Your Own in the Wilderness*. Stackpole, 1965.

You Alone in the Maine Woods. Augusta: Maine Dept. of Inland Fisheries and Game.

CHAPTER 2

That which does not kill us makes us stronger.

--F. W. Nietzsche.

THE VEHICLE AS A SURVIVAL DEVICE

Being stranded in a vehicle is not an uncommon occurrence in either the summer or winter. On major arteries help arrives quickly, but on back roads or even off the roads in back-country, it would not be unusual to spend some time waiting for assistance. Unless you are absolutely sure you can walk out quickly, it is best to stay with your car since searchers will likely find it much easier than a person on foot.

In cold weather, your best bet is to stay in the car where you have some protection from the elements. In warmer weather though, you may be able to stay outside of the car, or even under the car if excessive heat is a problem. If the bugs are bad though, you may wish to stay in a hot car rather than put up with the pests. If help is going to be sometime arriving, and if the situation is desperate, you may have to damage your vehicle in order to survive. As an example.

1.   Vinyl from seats, dashboards, and roofs can be used as insulation.

2.   The carpet from the trunk and the floors can be used as blanket or shelter material.

53

3.   If necessary, paneling and upholstery can be used to build a fire.

4.   In order to start a fire without matches, cross the positive and negative leads to the car battery in order to generate sparks. Collect these sparks in a gas-soaked rag lying on a metal hubcap; once the rag is on fire, carry the blaze to a pre-arranged fire site, conveniently situated close to the vehicle. (Extreme caution is suggested when starting fires in this manner, since the battery could explode.)

5.   Drinking water can be collected in taillight covers, hubcaps, windshield washer fluid containers, or even ashtrays.

6.   Burning oil, floor mats, tires and other rubber articles will produce a thick black smoke. This is an excellent way to attract attention.

7.   Mirrors can be used as reflecting devices in order to signal rescuers.

8.   A powerful signal lamp can be made simply by attaching the leads from headlights directly to the car battery.

9.   Wires can be made to serve as snare devices, fishing line, or various traps and hooks.

10.   Be sure that you equip your car with an emergency survival kit. The survival kit will enable you to spend time in modest comfort, rather than dangerous alarm.

VEHICULAR SURVIVAL KIT

All cars and trucks that travel our highways should carry a vehicular survival kit. Here are the items such a kit should carry:

EMERGENCY MECHANICAL EQUIPMENT
1.   Tool kit
2.   Jack (preferably a tri-pod type of jack)
3.   Strap-on tire chains
4.   Tow cable (wire rope, chain or heavy manilla rope)
5.   Jumper cables
6.   Shovel
7.   Tire inflator
8.   Gasoline can
9.   Siphon hose
10. Flashlight

11. Flares
12. Emergency reflectors
13. Spare fan belts
14. Gasoline de-icer
15. Canvas tarp or plastic sheet (3 m x 4 m)
16. Sheathed axe

EMERGENCY CLOTHING
A duffel bag for:
1. Heavy shirt
2. Wool pants
3. Hat
4. Heavy socks
5. Parka
6. Serviceable boots
7. Rain gear
8. Pair of mitts or gloves
9. Sleeping bag

Anyone motoring through wilderness areas should pack a vehicular survival kit.

EMERGENCY FOOD
1. Into a metal pot (for boiling water), place:
2. Matches (water proof)
3. Candles (carry four or five)
4. Packaged soups
5. Oxo cubes
6. Raisins
7. Cup
8. Nuts

STALLED VEHICLE IN THE COLD

Beyond the hazard of driving on slick road surfaces, those who drive in cold environments face the possibility of becoming stuck in snowdrifts or stalled in a blizzard or a whiteout.

When any of these situations occur and help is not readily available, the first thought that comes to mind is to walk out for aid. While many have successfully reached help, walking over great distances under blizzard conditions may prove disastrous; it could well be the last walk the victim will ever make.
Some believe this only occurs in the far north! It can't happen in our region, they say. And yet, this attitude may very well have cost some people frostbitten limbs or in some cases, their lives.

Motorists are advised to seriously consider the dangers they might encounter while driving along winter roads.

What should the stranded motorist do if stuck and help is not forthcoming?

Analyze the situation, and ask the following questions: Will the weather, snow conditions, wind and visibility permit the walk?; Will the remaining daylight permit me to reach help?; Is the clothing I have with me adequate for cold weather travel?; and Am I physically in condition for walking out?

The answers to these questions must all be positive. One negative or questionable answer and all a person may have going for him is luck. Therefore, remain in the car, and be thankful for the survival kit in the trunk. (See list of items to include in emergency kit.) If no immediate danger exists, relax, take a deep breath, and set about your tasks.

First, set out emergency reflectors. Take out of the trunk all usable items: rugs, mats, rags, cardboard, sacks, bags, and suitcases. Using the shovel, "bank" the car with snow. Don't forget the underside of the car. This will provide some degree of insulation.

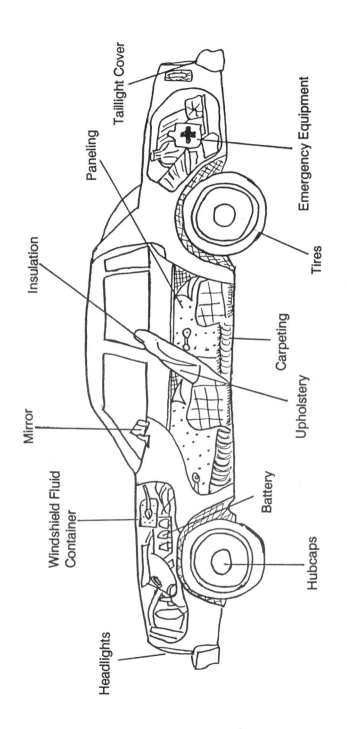

Taillight Cover

Emergency Equipment

Paneling

Tires

Insulation

Carpeting

Upholstery

Mirror

Windshield Fluid
Container

Battery

Hubcaps

Headlights

Also, on occasion, turn on the inside dome light to make the vehicle more visible to road crews or rescue parties. Turn hazard flashing lights on if approaching vehicles are heard.

Place a lighted candle, if possible, up by the windshield to act as a beacon. Incidentally, recent research has proven that lit candles do not effectively heat a vehicle unless car is fully insulated (banked) with snow.

Using the rugs, mats, cardboard, and any extra clothing, insulate the exposed glass and metal parts of the car. Open a vent in the car. Relax. Put on some extra clothes from the emergency survival kit.

Using extra mats, seatcovers, rags or clothing, make a snug little "bed" in the back seat. Keep off the lower area; stay as high as possible, since this is where heat will accumulate. The victim should loosen any tight, restricting garments that might hinder blood circulation including tight pants, pantyhose, and nylon stockings.

Do not "sit" on your legs; sit in a curled-up position. If vehicle has been thoroughly insulated, there should not be any need to run the car's engine; besides, the gasoline will be needed and a running car could result in carbon monoxide poisoning and a run down battery.

If vehicle is in a badly exposed and dangerous section of highway, the driver may be better off making a shelter in the woods reasonably close to the vehicle. The added protection provided by trees will undoubtedly make the victim's predicament a less stressful experience.

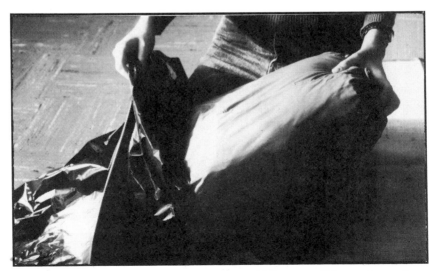

Always equip your vehicle for winter driving conditions. A good sleeping bag is mandatory.

People who have been stranded can testify that steel conducts heat many times faster than still air. For example, if a car and a snow shelter were compared, both in still air, the automobile would conduct heat away as much as 1900 times faster than the shelter. Aircraft bodies of aluminum alloy conduct heat even faster. If temperatures are cold, the stranded motorist is advised to insulate the entire vehicle with snow.

As a safety measure, tie bright strips of cloth on saplings, and place these poles around the car. Attach more cloth on the antenna and any other object protruding from the vehicle. This precaution will warn motorists (and snowplows) of the vehicle's existence.

In many cases, vehicles becoming stalled or stranded could have been prevented.

Often, the driver is totally unprepared for winter roads and conditions, or neglects to slow down when approaching whiteouts. Furthermore, too many winter motorists routinely drive with their heaters on full blast, do not wear protective clothing such as coats, mitts, or boots, and do not have ready access to their vehicle emergency kits.

Our advice is to turn down the heater and to dress warmly when driving on highways. Should the car leave the roadway, a sudden drop in temperature will not place the victim in a state of shock.

The following cold weather vehicle tips might prevent someone from becoming stranded on the frozen highway:

A. Fan belts occasionally break in the cold weather. A strong cord around the drive shaft and water pump pullies, tied with a simple square knot will get the motorist to the nearest station. Leave out the alternator pully or this emergency repair will not work. All electrical equipment not needed for travel should be turned off.

B. Remove some air out of the tires. If stuck in sand, mud or snow, the larger contact area with the ground tends to reduce slippage.

C. Push twigs, small branches, loose gravel or snow chains under, in front of and behind stuck tires to reduce tire slippage. Anything that increases friction will create a better surface for tires to grip. Some winter motorists carry strips of old carpet and use these for extra traction.

D. If a 4-wheel drive vehicle gets stuck and the drive wheels on either end lose traction, slowly press the accelerator and steady the foot brakes. This puts a load on the spinning wheel and transfers power to the wheel with possibly better traction. Also do the same thing with a 2-wheel drive vehicle - gently apply the parking brakes.

E. When highways are covered with fine snow, remove foot off the accelerator when approaching oncoming vehicles, especially larger trucks. Be prepared to stop. The blowing snow caused by moving air produces momentary blizzard conditions and zero visibility. Occasionally, this powdery snow can cause the engine to stall. It enters the air cleaner and blocks the supply of oxygen to the engine. Remove the air cleaner cartridge and brush out the snow.

F. If temperature is below zero, do not set emergency brakes overnight. They may freeze to the brake drums. If very cold, park your car on rubber mats or old strips of carpet to keep the tires from freezing to the ground.

Motorists can't control or predict the weather. They can, however, concentrate on safe, cautious, and courteous driving. They should be willing to slow down and offer assistance to any stranded people. During the winter months, there is no place for the impatient driver, especially on frozen highways.

At first glance, these safety precautions might seem too detailed and difficult to follow. Some might question the need to pack all of the suggested equipment in their trunks. This may be very well true; however, it is only your life...and that should be a very sobering thought.

It may become necessary for the stranded motorist to construct a shelter in the nearby bush. Prior to abandoning vehicle, leave a note stating direction of travel.

SURVIVAL KITS

Most avid outdoorspeople are proud of their individual survival kits. When asked to display them, they often reach into large knapsacks or waterproof canoe packs and pull out tiny plastic containers with the mandatory contents: snare wire, fishline and hooks, a small knife, a compass, and some matches. Regardless of the fact that very few people possess the skill and knowledge to utilize these meager objects under highly stressful situations, some individuals have great expectations of survival kits. In many cases, kits may offer a false sense of security.

Firstly, how many have truly tested the reliability of survival kits, even under controlled circumstances? Chances are that although we have them on hand, rarely are survival kits used under trying circumstances.

Secondly, too few individuals have the expertise to effectively use a kit's contents. Stating that a match and a knife are all one needs to live in our forests is a fool's notion of wilderness survival. Although we do not permit even these paultry items in our survival courses, the reader should understand that the student is gradually brought to this level of self-reliance. To give nothing to any neophyte and expect him to survive is sheer nonsense!

Thirdly, a survival kit occasionally offers a false sense of security. For example, some sportsmen take unnecessary chances when travelling through isolated areas. They leave their gear in any given spot and travel further, thinking that they'll return later and pick up their equipment. In a small container, however, they'll carry a survival kit; the logic seems sound: in case of emergency, the survival kit is on hand; therefore, nothing to worry about! Little do these people realize that without proper training, a survival kit is next to useless. Attempting to cope with bugs, torrential rains, freezing temperatures, or cold nights without proper gear and training is enough to drive anyone insane.

True wilderness survival training eliminates any false sense of security. Instead, it highlights the survivor's real survival kit: his brain. Using whatever is available, including a survival kit, the victim looks not at what he doesn't have, but to what nature is willing to offer. In short, mosses and bark become roofing material; pyrites are turned into firestarters; boughs, when properly prepared and handled, become a soft bed.

Fourthly, most survival kits are carried in knapsacks. Should the victim become separated from his sack, he loses his kit! A canoe tips over and everything is lost. Furthermore, many kits are so compact, and sealed in such a manner that they are almost impossible to open, even under the best of conditions.

Finally, we come to the question of accessibility. Wilderness survival is not normally a planned, ordered, or normal activity. Either through poor planning or just plain bad luck, a victim finds himself in dire straits. Under these circumstances, where should the survival kit be located? In a separate container, near but not in the knapsack? Strapped to one's belt? We are convinced that all items required to successfully survive a night or two in the wilderness should be safely, effectively, and conveniently carried in one's clothing. If the victim is properly dressed for wilderness travel, his clothes are loose, bulky, and contain many pockets. Vests, army pants and jackets are ideal for housing a personal survival kit.

We advise wilderness travellers to carry:

1. high quality pocket knife
2. compass
3. waterproof container with matches (waterproofed) and a metal match
4. needles and thread
5. snare wire - 5 metres
6. personal medicines
7. 2 large green garbage bags; space blanket
8. 10 large bandaids
9. insect repellent
10. safety pins - 1 dozen
11. small steel signalling mirror
12. some dried foods, soups, and nuts
13. small metal cup
14. writing equipment (in waterproof container)
15. survival book (in waterproof container)

All fifteen items can be easily carried in a multi-pocketed vest and a good pair of army pants.

Properly trained and bush-wise individuals realize the importance of all these items. In addition, the knife, compass, and cup are attached to fairly long, colourful string or laniard. In the event that they're dropped, the colourful string makes them easier to find. Also, if some binding has to be done, this string is readily available.

The waterproof match container can be old 35 mm film canisters. They're waterproof, float, and are easily opened. Matches should be the strike anywhere variety, and completely dipped in nail polish remover or paraffin wax. If hunting, the sportsman is advised to place a few matches in the butt end of his gun, that is, in the space normally reserved for his cleaning kit.

We include writing equipment in our survival kit. If lost or stranded, the victim is advised to write his emotions, feelings, and activities. In so doing, he'll calm down. A calm person is less prone to succumb to panic. Also, should the victim decide to leave his shelter, a note can be left behind in the event a search party locates the old site.

The survival book offers some reading material, thereby keeping his mind occupied and active. It may even offer some worthwhile advice. If nothing else, the book can become kindling or toilet paper!

The cup being metal, becomes a small pot in which to prepare hot soups.

We suggest that each survival kit contain two large garbage bags. In the event of an emergency, the victim can sleep in one. Meanwhile, the other, once split, becomes a quick, rainproof roof to a small A-Frame shelter, or a ground sheet. The space blanket can also be used for this purpose.

Others believe that a good survival kit should be carried in a small pack sack. This school of thought recommends placing everything in a sealed metal container. A small blanket, wrapped in garbage bags is also included in the sack. In the event of an emergency, the metal container becomes a pot, while the blanket, when fitted inside the garbage container, becomes a sleeping bag.

Although we prefer to have a kit inside our pockets, others rely on the packsack approach. Individuals who fall in this category should ask themselves the following questions:
1. Does my kit float?
2. Is it compact, manageable, lightweight, and easily portable?
3. Are the contents accessible under adverse conditions?
4. Can I get to it quickly?

If all answers are positive, great! If not, seriously reconsider another type of survival kit. In any case, we urge all outdoors people to experiment, and devise some type of kit which best suits their needs.

SEARCH AND RESCUE

Knowing and understanding how search and rescue organization function could conceivably aid the victim to be found...if (s)he knows what to expect. Rescue may be defined as the act of offering assistance or aiding someone in trouble, i.e. someone who cannot assist himself/herself. Under such circumstances, the victim is generally isolated and cannot correct his/her predicament alone.

THE SEARCH PATROL

One of the many differences between an organized and a disorganized search lies in the functioning of the search patrol. A significant amount of time and effort can be saved by an intelligent and co-ordinated use of men and equipment; this is what the search patrol is intended to provide.

No search patrol can be organized without some trained and experienced personnel in its makeup. Because of the varied nature of their regular occupations, not all experienced members are present at any given search, while a number of untrained volunteers may be available; however, knowledgeable members usually stand ready to assume, at one time or another, some of the key positions in a patrol.

Stated very simply, the one and only objective of the search patrol is to find a lost person or persons by working as systematically and efficiently as possible. Anything which contributes to systematic searching is good; anything which hinders, prevents, or distracts from an efficient search is counter-productive. The main purpose of a search patrol is to do a difficult job as well as humanly possible because a person's life may and frequently does, depend upon how well it is done.

Many Search and Rescue Units do not operate with permanently-assigned patrols. Instead, patrols are formed on an ad hoc basis as dictated by the needs and conditions of each search. Factors such as terrain, time, weather, and availability of manpower will differ considerably from one search to another. Thus, not all that follows will be rigidly adhered to on every search, but the general principles involved remain constant:

1. Personnel
   A normal search patrol consists of 4 to 8 persons. It includes:

Patrol Leader: a fully-trained and experienced searcher appointed by the Area Commander and acting on his instructions. He is able to interpret these instructions, to provide leadership, and to assign tasks within the patrol.

Patrol Second: a fully-trained and experienced searcher is appointed by the patrol leader and capable of taking over from him if the need arises.

Compass Bearer: responsible for keeping a continuous check on patrol direction with respect to assigned compass bearings.

Pacer: responsible for keeping a continuous check on the distance travelled by the patrol.

Radio man: responsible for maintaining communication with base via portable radio unit.

All patrol members, including those not assigned specific tasks, normally keep a fairly regular personal check on compass direction and distance travelled.

The key man in the patrol is the patrol leader. He is responsible to the Area Commander for the safe and efficient functioning of the group of searchers which he leads. Before setting out, he obtains the names of all members of his patrol, provides a full briefing, and assigns other duties. During the search, he endeavours to keep his own record of compass bearings and pacing; records the time, place, and probable significance of all potential signs of the lost person discovered en route; and maintains effective communications within his patrol and with base. On return to base, he reports to the Area Commander and does not dismiss his patrol until authorized to do so.

Because all members of most Search and Rescue Units are volunteers, and because non-members may occasionally be involved in searches, a well-functioning patrol requires tact, understanding, and full cooperation between the patrol leader and searchers. The leader tries to assess the strengths and weaknesses of the searchers under his command and acts accordingly. In all matters immediately affecting the patrol and its work, the patrol leader's judgement and decisions must be respected; he has the respectability, expertise, and experience; he must therefore have the authority.

2. Equipment
   Unit equipment (radios, ropes, first-aid kits, etc.) are returned to base stores at the end of the day. Personal equipment is the responsibility of the individual searcher. Any patrol member may carry as much as he wishes for personal use, but remember, to travel light is to travel easy; all searchers carry a good compass, a knife, a notebook and pencil, and personal food (sandwiches,

chocolate, etc.). Searchers usually wear some brightly coloured clothing so as to be easily seen in the bush.

SEARCH PROCEDURES

Once the base camp has been set up (and everyone helps with this) the Area Commander decides how best to deploy the manpower available. He then appoints and briefs patrol leaders, who, in turn, brief the members of their patrols. The information given in the briefing ensures that every patrol member knows the answers to the following questions before the patrol sets out:

WHY? Searchers are initiated by various official agencies (Military, City Police, etc.) and for various reasons. The patrol leader explains why the search is considered necessary by the authorities.

WHO? If the object of the search is a person, patrol members must know as much as possible about the person. Child or adult? Male or female? First and last names? Age? Height? Weight? Where last seen? When last seen? Physical condition prior to being lost? Survival supplies carried? Possess any survival knowledge? Clothing materials and colours? These are but a few points members of the search party must know.

Briefing members of the search party prior to departure.

If the object of the search is a vehicle, e.g. aircraft or boat, information such as the type, size, colour, departure and destination points, is given to the patrol.

WHEN? The timing of the various phases of the search operation is understood by all patrol members. Flexibility of plans may depend upon a knowledge of what other patrols are doing at a particular time. The expected duration of patrol sweeps may be very important in regard to rendezvous points, joint emergency action, etc.

WHERE? All patrol members are to know exactly where they are, and where they are going. They are shown the various positions on a map, and are able to form an accurate mental picture of the geography and topography of the area in which they will be working. Compass bearings, distances, rendezvous points, etc., are clearly understood by all.

During the briefing, all patrol members make notes concerning the above items for personal reference in the course of the search. Different circumstances and conditions require different types of patrol and search pattern. The following examples will illustrate some of the main types:

(a) 2-man probe or reconnaissance.
Such a patrol might be used in an attempt to intersect a lost person's trail or to check out a possible sighting. A 2-man group is the smallest ever employed in search operations and at least one person must be an experienced searcher. Never search alone - it is usually unprofitable and frequently unsafe.

Each searcher carefully examines all clues, including tracks and discarded objects. These are immediately reported to the patrol leader.

67

(b) Track Crawl.

A two or more man patrol following a road or truck checking for footprints and other signs and scanning the bush to a depth of 3-5 metres on either side.

(c) Lake Shore Reconnaissance.

A two or more man patrol to determine whether the lost person has visited or made camp by a lake. This is done by making a circuit of the lake either on shore or by canoe.

(d) 6 - 8 Man Sweep.

This is one of the most common forms of patrol used in bush search work. The patrol "sweeps" an area in line abreast with searchers 3 to 9 metres apart. The interval between searchers will vary according to the object of the search (a child, a downed aircraft, etc.) and the nature of the terrain (very dense bush, relatively open areas, etcs.). This type of patrol may include much larger numbers(e.g. 30 - 40 people) but the larger the patrol the greater the problems of maintaining line and interval because of communication difficulties.

Before setting out, the patrol leader makes clear the methods of communication and procedures to be followed once the sweep is under way. Some of these are:

(a) Numbering

When the patrol is lined out at its starting point it is advisable (especially with patrols of six or more) to have the members number from one end. Then, in the course of the sweep it is possible to establish the relative positions of all members of the patrol by asking them to "Nummmbbberrr!".

(b) Stopping and Starting in the Bush

When any member of the patrol wishes the patrol to stop for any reason, he shouts "Hold the Line!" and all members halt where they are. When the patrol is ready to move on again, the patrol leader shouts "Let's go!" or "Move out!".

(c) Unnecessary Noise

Aside from the above instances, patrol members do not shout unnecessarily during the sweep. Shouting may confuse other members of the patrol or mislead other patrols operating in the area and may prevent searchers from hearing the calls of a lost person.

(d) Maintaining Line and Interval

In order to ensure adequate coverage of the area being searched, it is important that the patrol line remain straight and the interval between searchers fairly constant. Each patrol member is able to see the man on either side throughout the sweep.

(e) Speed

The speed of the patrol is always the speed of its slowest member and in searching, the slowest member may be the most efficient searcher. Simply walking through dense bush is a job in itself, but doing so while keeping to a compass course, maintaining line and interval, and carefully searching for any sign of a lost person is not a job to be rushed at. A search is not a race in which prizes are won for being first past the post.

The only reward is finding the lost person; proceeding methodically and carefully is the only way to be reasonably sure of achieving this end result.

(f) Clues and Signs

Any sign that might be relevant to the lost person is investigated. The searcher shouts "Hold the Line", checks out the sign without disturbing it, and reports it at once to the patrol leader if it appears significant. Significant signs might be footprints, signs of campfire or resting place, bleeding, bowel or bladder evacuation, torn particles of clothing, cigarette butts, broken twigs to trampled grass, and food wrappings.

(g) Dividing a Patrol During a Sweep

It may be necessary in certain circumstances for the patrol leader to divide the patrol into two or more groups in the course of a sweep. In such instances, no group is less than two men and base camp is informed of such changes immediately. No searcher leaves the patrol without the knowledge and permission of the patrol leader; he is "signed out".

The victim might blaze his trail using trees, branches or rocks.

69

In summary, the keys to success are (a) objectives which are clearly stated and generally understood; (b) organization, which combines (c) good communications, (d) discipline, (e) flexibility, and (f) optimum use of experienced manpower; and (g) procedures which ensure coordinated and effective action in the field. Search patrols, as the living embodiments of these ideas, may not always produce the desired results, but they will at least as often as any other method.

SUGGESTED READING

Blodget, R. "Survival in the North." *Flying*, 1967, 80: 40-41.

Craighead, F.C. and John, J.J., *How to Survive on Land and Sea*. Maryland: United States Naval Institute.

Douglas and McIntyre. *Outdoor Safety and Survival*. Vancouver: Douglas and McIntyre, 1984.

Ferri, G.F. "The Best Survival Kit." *Angler & Hunter*, July, 1988, p. 30.

Ferri, G. F. "Don't Get Stuck Out In The Cold." *Leisure World*, December, 1989, p. 22-23

Hatton, M. *Lightweight Camping*. Toronto: Humber College Press, 1981.

Houser, D.G. "Could You Survive a Wilderness Emergency?" *Adventure Travel*, May, 1980, 24-27.

Johnston, Don. *Lakehead Search and Rescue Training Handbook*. Thunder Bay: L.S. and R.U., 1982.

Mayday, Mayday, Mayday. C.F.P. 1-OA-143-001/TS-001, Ottawa: Information Canada, 1978.

Nesbitt, P. H., Pond, A. W., Allen, W.H. *The Survival Book.* New York: Van Nostrand, 1972.

Palmer, E.L. *Survival in Winter*. Cooperative Extension Service, Cornell University, 1952.

Poynter, M. *Search and Rescue*. New York: McClelland & Stewart, 1980.

Robbins, R. *Mantracking*. Montrose: Search and Rescue Magazine, 1977.

Rutstrum, C. *Paradise Below Zero*. New York: Collier Book, 1972.

Setnicka, T. J. *Wilderness Search and Rescue.* Boston: Appalachian Mtn Club, 1980.

West Virginia Bureau of Highway Safety Promotion. *Blizzard: Safety and Survival*, 1968.

CHAPTER 3

Nothing will ever be attempted if all possible objections must first be overcome.

Clement

FIRE LORE

The earliest uses humans made of fire were to shed light and to keep warm. Today, we find fire a useful survival tool for the same purposes. There are many examples of people dying in survival situations because they were not able to get a fire started. In order to survive, one must master the techniques of starting, building and maintaining a fire should a mishap occur.

FIRE - THE MORALE BOOSTER

Fires help the stranded member solve many of the problems he may face while undergoing an emergency situation in arctic-like areas of the world. Warmth, light, drying clothing and equipment, melting snow or ice for water, cooking plants or animals for food, morale, and signalling to attract the attention of Search and Rescue groups are all dependent, to a degree, upon the survivor's ability to produce and maintain a fire of some sort.

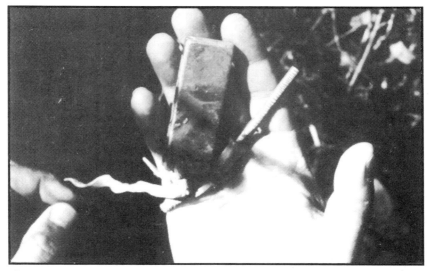

Contrary to public opinion, a magnesium stick (or metal match) offers the survivor a relatively simple and effective method of starting fires without matches.

Fire is the heat and light that comes from burning substances. Three conditions must co-exist before fire can be produced and maintained:

a) there must be a fuel or material that will burn;

b) there must be heat enough to bring the material to its kindling point (temperature at which oxygen will rapidly unite with the fuel); and

c) there must be plenty of oxygen, which normally comes from ambient air.

These conditions are commonly referred to as the fire triangle. If any one of these conditions is not fulfilled, there can be no fire.

Fires may be one of two common classes: solids and liquids. Solid fuels are usually most common in survival firecraft. Wood can be found in most North American areas. The burning of solid fuel often depends on its form. One may not be able to ignite a large log with a match but a small twig from the same log may catch fire easily with the same match. This is because the twig has more oxygen (air) available in proportion to the fuel (wood) to be burned, therefore less heat (the match) is required. This explains why it is easy to start a fire using splinters of shavings.

Liquid fuels - include gasoline and oils from a car or aircraft, canned heat from survival kits, and animal fats. Normally these are easily burned. Oxygen is taken from the air in and around the fire. If there is not enough oxygen, the fire will die. You may have to fan or re-arrange a fire to create drafts so that an ample amount of oxygen is available. By doing this you can make your fire "come to life" again.

Fire, besides providing heat and light, is a morale booster to the stranded survivor.

Personal survival kits should contain one or more fire starting devices:

a) matches - one of the easiest and most effective fire starters; good to carry them in water-tight container.

b) cigarette lighters - keep warm - do not throw away, since they can be used to spark a fire (see unit on charred cloth).

c) metal match or flint - producing sparks to ignite fire.

d) candles - True, they must be ignited by other means. Once lighted, however, they provide a more intense heat and will burn for a longer period of time than the device used to light them. The candle is a fire in itself. The heat, light, drying ability, cooking capabilities, and value as a signalling device may be limited - but they should not be overlooked by the survivor!

FIRE MAKING

Look for rock, gravel or sand on which to build your fire, then clear the area around it of all flammable material to make sure the fire can't spread. Never build a fire at the base of a tree, or near enough for heat to kill the roots. Prepare tinder, kindling and fuel and make exactly the kind of fire you need.

FIRE MAKERS

The best are large wooden matches; waterproof in paraffin or nailpolish remover. Dip entire match, including wooden section.

NATURAL FIRE STARTERS

Use natural tinders for fire starters. Bark from a birch is excellent. Dry wood stalks and tiny twigs from evergreen trees make good fire starters. Be certain such stalks and twigs are dead and dry.

FIRE WOOD: KINDLING

Kindling should be of good dry sticks and twigs graduated in size from pieces just bigger than tinder up to pieces as thick as a thumb, and from 10 to 20 centimetre long. Longer pieces may be split for kindling. Dead conifer branches are good for fuel. This is called 'squaw-wood'; it is the kind Native women used to collect. Break the sticks into suitable lengths and sort them out - thin sticks for quick fires, thick for slow fires. Split logs burn faster than whole logs.

STARTING A FIRE - A FOUNDATION

For an easy fire, lay the squaw-wood over two other sticks, so that the wind will help the blaze by blowing through the fire when lighted. Do this by having the wind at your back, as you face the fire. Place the tinder under the squaw-wood. Place thin sticks and finally somewhat larger sticks over the squaw-wood. Light the tinder, putting the flame under the center of the pile of tinder, breaking the match to make certain that it is out or throw it in the fire. As the flame catches and begins to spread, add bits of tinder, placing them gently on the flame until there is a brisk fire.

FIRE WOOD

Dry wood burns better than green wood. A great amount of heat is lost in drying the water out of the green wood before the wood begins to burn. Hickory is the best wood to use. Willow is rated as fair for quick and slow fires, while cottonwood is poor. The following are some hints for collecting wood. Wood for kindling should snap when broken. Tinder may be anything that is very light and dry - not to be any thicker than a match. Make little bundles of tiny twigs. Sticks that bend and do not snap are green; use these only after a hot fire is started. Wood that crumbles is rotten. It has lost all its life and will just smoulder and smoke without giving off any heat. Split wood burns well; the inside of a log is drier than the outside. Soft wood is from quick growing trees. It is good for starting fires, or for quick hot fires. It burns up quickly and needs constant refueling; it does not leave good coals. Hard wood is produced by trees that grow slowly. It is compact and firm, and feels heavy in the hand as compared with a piece of soft wood of the same size. This kind of wood burns slowly, and yields coals that will last. It needs a good hot fire to get started, and then burns well for a long time.

Squaw-wood, the lower dead branches of coniferous trees, contain a great deal of resin. They will burn even when damp. Combined with Birch bark, squaw-wood is undoubtedly the best kindling found in the wilds.

SOME TINDER MATERIALS

Dried grass
- Cattail fluff
- Dried, crushed nettles
- Dead, dry burs (Burdock)
- Milkweed fluff
- Shredded Cedar/Juniper bark
- Finely shredded birch bark
- Bird nests
- Fireweed fluff
- Burned or charred materials; e.g. charred cloth (especially cotton), charred wood remnants from forest fires and charred punkwood.
- Fungus *Fomes fomentarius*, a bracket-type species usually found growing on dead Birch trees. Dry out fungus, later pounding into a fine powder. This powder makes an ideal base for catching sparks.
- Dried, finely crushed mullein leaves.

Old bird nests make excellent tinder.

We advise the stranded victim to initially harvest wood that is a fair distance from his shelter. As he weakens, he can gather wood closer to the survival site.

Heat to a survivor in cold climate is a thing of joy. Common sense is sometimes forgotten and the use of fires becomes a careless operation. Clothes are burned when drying, cooking pots and other equipment are scorched and ruined. Survivors are burned. Fire must be treated with respect and good common sense:

a) do not build a fire too close to your shelter - flying sparks could conceivably set roof boughs aflame;

b) if a fire is to be inside the shelter, keep it small and under control. Ventilate to guard against carbon monoxide poisoning; and

c) in the open, fires merely create drafts. Position your fire near a sheltered stone reflector.

SUMMARY

Tinder: Bark from cedar, birch, basswood or elm trees;
          Weed tops from goldenrod, aster, milkweed or cattail;
          Very small dry twigs.

Kindling: Dead evergreen twigs, squaw-wood: the lower dead branches of
          conifers; (if you can't snap it, scrap-it; however, remember, in winter,
          even live twigs will snap, so use your common sense)
          Willow, alder and aspen

Abandoned nest of the Paper Wasp is also excellent tinder material.

Fuel: Thumb-thick branches to heavy logs - dry wood preferably; if a long-lasting, smoky fire is desired, use green wood. Hardwood - trees that grow slowly; heavy; burn slowly; these trees usually shed leaves during winter.
Softwood - trees grow quickly; light in weight; burn very quickly; evergreens.

Make sure you have tinder, kindling and plenty of fuel; a spot has been cleared for your fire - all set to begin making your fire.

TEEPEE FIRE - THE OLD DEPENDABLE

Place a handful of tinder on the ground. Push a stick into the ground on a slant over the tinder. Now lean a circle of kindling sticks across the slanting stick with their tips together and with an opening towards the wind. Set kindling afire with your back to the wind.

CRISS/CROSS FIRE - ANOTHER TRADITIONAL

Place two pieces of wood as thick as your wrist and 30 cm in length on the ground, parallel to one another, approximately 30 cm apart. Lay a number of thin kindling sticks crosswise on top of the base between each stick. Continue building up cross

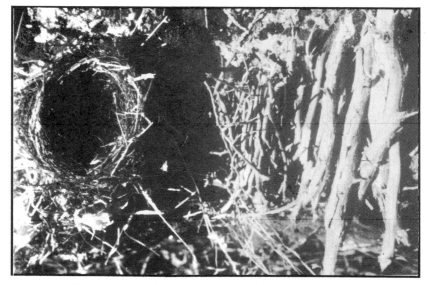

Order of burning firewood: tinder, kindling, logs.

layers increasing the thickness of the wood from layer to layer. Light tinder near ground from windward side.

SOME EMERGENCY FIRE STARTING TECHNIQUES

Much has been written about the lunacy of attempting to start fires without the use of matches. Many experts maintain that no one should venture into the wilderness without matches (a suggestion we also espouse); hence, they say, no one needs to know other fire making techniques. Others claim that learning non-traditional firestarting techniques is a waste of time, since a great deal of skill, patience, and expertise is normally required to start any fire without the use of matches. Of course, anyone can argue, firestarting with proper matches or a lighter is relatively simple compared to, let us say, the firebow!

Our stand, however, is radically different!

We do not claim that mastering the firebow technique, or the use of flint and steel, is a simple process as some manuals would have us believe. It's a very difficult, complicated, and frustrating skill to master, even under ideal conditions. Why then, discuss emergency fire starting techniques? Quite simple - the survivor must strive

Using leverage, snap firewood into manageable lengths.

to utilize every conceivable avenue to insure that a fire is present at his site. Otherwise, what is he to do - give up?

The psychological realities of survival dictate that the victim utilize every available technique to create fire! The following firestarting methods may be, comparatively speaking, difficult to master. Also, some of the materials mentioned are difficult to obtain. We do not deny these realities. On the other hand, the more ways an individual knows (and masters), the better his/her chances of surviving a wilderness ordeal.

MAGNESIUM STICK (OR METAL MATCH)

This handy devise is a mere 10 cm long and 2 cm wide. It fits easily into any pocket, survival kit, or on a key chain, and is readily available at most hardware stores.

The magnesium stick (sometimes called a metal match) requires a minimum amount of practice to master, and produces a shower of sparks with little effort. Simply draw the blade of your pocket knife (or for that matter, any hard, sharp edge such as stone, glass, or metal) over the side of the magnesium stick. To maximize the full impact of resulting sparks, shave small particles of magnesium from the metal match, and add to a prepared pile of kindling.

As many can testify, the sparks alone do not produce fire; they need dry tinder on which to land. There are many sources of tinder in the bush: cattail fluff, finely shredded birch and cedar bark, ground-up bracket fungus, and dried out punkwood.

Some tinder materials may be found in one's camping gear - very fine steel wool is great - lightweight and compact. So is cotton and charred cloth!

Another method is to smash branches against a tree or rock; they'll snap where hit. If unable to break, burn log in half or feed one end into the fire.

81

We advise the neophyte to hold the magnesium stick close to the tinder, thereby enabling more sparks to land into the prepared "nest". Gently blow into the smoldering tinder to produce a flame.

CARBIDE

Carbide is a greyish-white material resembling crushed shale or slate. When dry, it is inactive. However, when in contact with moisture, the resulting gas becomes extremely volatile and flammable.

There are two basic ways to use this mineral as an emergency fire starter:

1. Obtain a small metal container. Empty shoe polish cans are ideal. Punch a small hole on top of the can. Add a few drops of water, barely enough to cover the bottom of the container. Throw in a chunk of carbide. Close the container. Wait for approximately thirty (30) seconds. This enables the gas to fill the entire container. Using a metal match, create a spark near the hole. A blue flame will soon shoot up. Light your kindling.

Caution -
(a)   if the survivalist does not wait the suggested thirty (30) seconds period to throw a spark, the enclosed gas, mixed with oxygen, has the nasty tendency to EXPLODE!
(b)   the liquid residue remaining at the bottom of the metal container is DEADLY POISONOUS.
            If any gets onto your skin, wash off immediately!

2. If a container is not available, make a small, enclosed cup (clay, mud, damp soil) on the ground, somewhat resembling and same size as a small cupped hand. In the centre, add a little moisture. Throw in the carbide. Wait 30 seconds. Using a metal match, create a spark. A small flame will soon result. Light your kindling (I strongly advise milkweed fluff).

Historically, the carbide and water flame was used by the early miners to light their hard-hat lamps.

POTASSIUM PERMANGANATE

This chemical should be in every outdoorperson's gear, especially those who do a fair amount of camping during the winter months. In its crystal form, potassium permanganate is dark red, somewhat purplish in colour. If water is added (or thrown on white snow) the resulting bright red dye can be seen from great distances.

To use as a fire starter, mix one part potassium permanganate to two parts sugar (sugar is not absolutely necessary; it serves to prolong the flame).

Carve a small, round hole (1 cm x 1 cm x 1 cm) in a chunk of wood. Place the mixture in this small hole. Using a solid stick the size of a pencil, grind the mixture. A flame will soon result. Have kindling readily available, since the flame is short lived.

FLINT AND STEEL

Hold the flint in your left hand with the tinder (charred cloth) pinched on top. Make sure that the sharp edge is tipped upward slightly, and strike a glancing downward blow with your steel. The sparks will be thrown upwards and caught by the tinder. Keep practicing; it will come. The steel can be in any form, preferably a cheap variety ie. not treated. Common sources include knives, belt buckles, car materials, etc. The rocks should be hard, silicate-containing, e.g. metamorphic and igneous rocks. If not sharp, break to create sharp edges. Good rocks include:
- flint: Utah, Ohio, Danish, Gunflint (found in Canadian Shield)
- Jasper
- Chert
- Quartz
- Feldspar

All can give off hot sparks and are found in many parts of Canada.

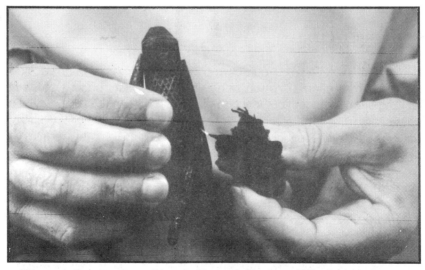

Although fire starting with a knife and flint is a difficult technique to master, once learned, this method is a reliable way of lighting fires without matches.

Iron ore, pyrite, and silver do not require metallic objects to spark. If struck against themselves or other hard minerals, sparks will result.

Once the spark has ignited the tinder, place the smoldering materials into a nest of dead, dried grass, shredded birch bark, and very small twigs. Blow the glowing tinder until flames ignite the nest.

MAKING FIRE WITH FLINT AND STEEL

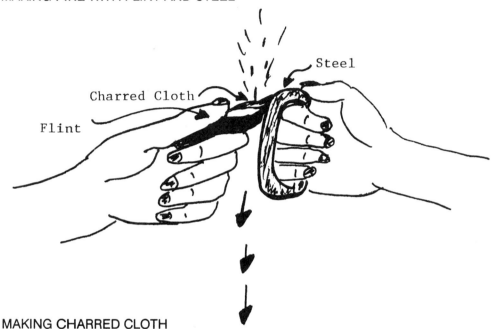

MAKING CHARRED CLOTH

One of the best materials the outdoors-person can have is charred cloth. This substance is simple charred cotton, linen or denim which, once a spark hits, will smolder long enough to get your kindling blazing. It is especially handy when trying to catch a spark from a metal match, flint and steel or firebow. So long as it is kept dry, charred cloth will keep indefinitely.

To make your own charred cloth, cut a piece of old 100% cotton T-shirt (synthetics don't char - they melt) or denim jeans into 3 cm x 3 cm strips. An old shoe polish tin that has been cleaned out will serve as a container. Make a hole in the top of the lid. Loosely jam these strips into the can. Shut the can tight! By placing the can into the fire, (or on a stove element) the cloth will char. Don't be alarmed to see flames emerge from the hole. This is an indication that the cloth is actually charring. After a few minutes, remove the can from the heat and let cool. If the cloth is black and crumbles easily, it is done. If not, repeat the procedure.

OTHER TINDER MATERIALS

In an emergency, suitable tinder can be made from dried tree fungus, dry, rotted wood (punkwood), dried puff balls, and dried, fluffed cattail tops. Incidentally, punkwood can be charred in the same fashion as cotton.

Dried, dead burrs can be fashioned into a small "nest". Once a spark is caught in charred cloth, quickly place it in the "nest". Blow hard! A flame will soon result. Remember to have all kindling and plenty of firewood ready before any attempt is made to start a fire.

BATTERIES AND STEEL WOOL

Sparks from a car battery can be used to start a fire in a similar fashion, e.g. cross wires! Furthermore, regular cell batteries can produce sparks, but fine steel wool is needed. By connecting the two 9-volt batteries as shown in the diagram, a stronger current is created.   A 20 cm roll of fine steel wool, rubbed gently at one end while other end is firmly held in place (see diagram) causes the current to ignite the steel wool. However, the batteries, being severely drained by this act, become drained almost immediately.   This method of firestarting is a one-shot deal. The drained batteries may not provide the victim with another chance. Ignited steel wool can be placed directly on kindling.

Emergency fire starting method with batteries and steel wool. This same principle can be applied to the car battery. By connecting the two terminals, the steel wool will ignite.

The aforementioned techniques of firestarting involve items which may be found in the camper's knapsack or first aid kit. Potassium permanganate could turn up in a medical kit; batteries, in a flashlight; steel wool, in the cooking gear; while most campers have access to a small metallic item such as a pocket knife. In short, the thinking, rational victim could start a fire using some of his equipment.

FIRE MAKING WITH BATTERIES AND STEEL WOOL

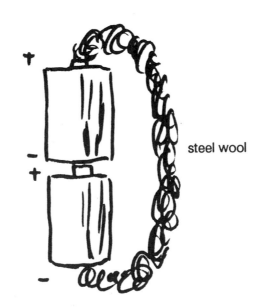

steel wool

Connect two batteries. Rub
steel wool gently on one end of battery.

FIREARM AND AMMUNITION

According to reliable statistics, hunters form the largest group (56%) of individuals which become lost in our forests. Hunters are the main utilizers of wilderness areas during autumn, and, as such, comprise the largest proportion of lost victims. Given these circumstances, we encourage all hunters to carry extra waterproof matches in the butt end of their guns, that is, in the space normally reserved for cleaning kits. If your rifle does have this space, throw in a few tightly wrapped matches. If your rifle is always with you, you are guaranteed a fire.

Guns can be utilized as firestarters in another manner. Carefully remove the projectile from its casing. This is done by placing the projectile's tip into the barrel. Using leverage and some gentle pressure, slowly loosen the tip. Be extremely careful not to damage the casing or spill gunpowder into the barrel. Once the projectile is removed, pour 90% of the powder onto a dry piece of Birch bark.

Into the almost empty casing, pack some loose and shredded 2 cm x 2 cm pieces of dry cotton. Fire into the air. With practise, the small amount of powder serves to ignite the cotton. Place the burning cloth into a prepared tinder nest and blow gently.

The remaining powder can be utilized in two ways. One is by slowly adding small amounts to the charred cotton. This encourages the tinder to ignite. Otherwise, a

Should the hunter lose his way in the forest, those few matches conveniently tucked in the butt end of his rifle might spare him a night of suffering.

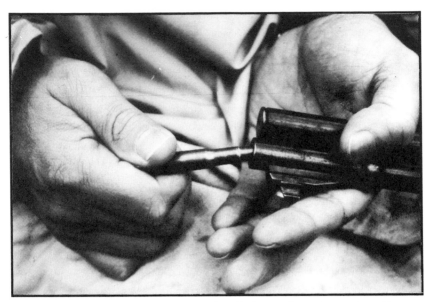

*Use the gun barrel to pry the projectile loose from its casing. Do so gently and carefully; take care not to damage casing or spill gunpowder. *Make certain firearm is unloaded.*

metal match is used to throw sparks directly into the pile of gunpowder. A searing hot, rapid flame will result.

Guns and ammunition are very effective firestarting devices; however, these techniques can also be very dangerous. The participant is strongly advised to make certain that his firearm is <u>unloaded</u> before commencing.

All these firestarting skills should be practised under the direct guidance of a trained and knowledgeable instructor.

THE FIREBOW

By far, the most primitive method of firestarting is with a firebow. This is a very difficult way to obtain fire, and should be used only when all other firestarting methods fail. For us, the firebow produces a fire six out of ten times, even though we have many years of experience; also, all the various factors affecting the efficiency of the firebow (i.e. proper woods used, dry climatic conditions, person is not exhausted, etc.) have been near perfect.

All the required materials needed to construct a firebow are available in the woods. Whether in the boreal forest, mixed woods, desert badlands, or coastal rainforests, all materials can be found, if the survivor knows what to look for!

All the required materials needed to construct a firebow are available in the woods. Whether in the boreal forest, mixed woods, desert badlands, or coastal rainforests, all materials can be found, if the survivor knows what to look for!

The firebow works as a result of the friction created when its parts rub against each other. The friction produces a hot dust which, when allowed to form a pile, can be blown into a cinder. Knowing this, one should first master easier methods of firestarting, and be efficient at collecting proper tinders so that the cinder created from the firebow can be transformed quickly into a flame. Experience has shown that since this firestarting technique is the most difficult of all, one must practice frequently and have great perseverance and patience.

FIREBOW - THE COMPONENTS

Socket -   Holds spindle in position while it's being turned; it is held in one hand and made from any piece of wood with a hollow on the underneath (some prefer a stone socket). The socket may be oiled or waxed, thus allowing the upper end of the drill to spin freely.

Spindle -   Should be as straight as possible 1-2 cm in diameter and approximately 12-16 cm long. Smooth out the top end as round as possible to minimize friction. The lower end, maximum of friction is wanted, therefore, make it as blunt and rough as possible.

Baseboards -Make by splitting a dry branch, approximately 2 cm thick, 6-7 cm wide and 30-40 cm long. Carve a hole 1 cm from the edge of the board. Hole should match (fit) the end of the spindle (blunt end). Notch from the edge of the fire board to the hole, making it wider and deeper at the bottom. This will allow the "hot black powder" that is produced by the drilling to fall into tinder massed at the bottom of the notch.

The Bow -   Any green piece of wood, approximately 2-3 cm in diameter and approximately 40-50 cm long. Bow string - anything ranging from shoe laces to twisted raw hide, tied at both ends of the bow; leave enough slack to allow its being twisted once around the spindle.

PUTTING IT TOGETHER

Find flat, sturdy ground surface on which to place baseboard. Make certain that ground is dry; otherwise, add several layers of flat birch bark pieces under the baseboard. Have twigs, tinder and wood on hand before starting to use the firebow. Place spindle in bow, as seen in diagram (a); using the top block, press down on spindle, but not enough to slow it. Begin "sawing" the spindle back and forth with the bow, using a steady, rhythmic pace. Work bow faster, never stopping the smooth, swift action. Hot black powder will be produced.

Once an ember is glowing, blow softly into notch until it glows; use it to get a fire started.

If spindle seems to "squeek" while being turned, stop working. Rough up bottom end and start again. In most cases, the best cinders are produced when a soft, grinding sound is heard.

FIRE BOW

The Components

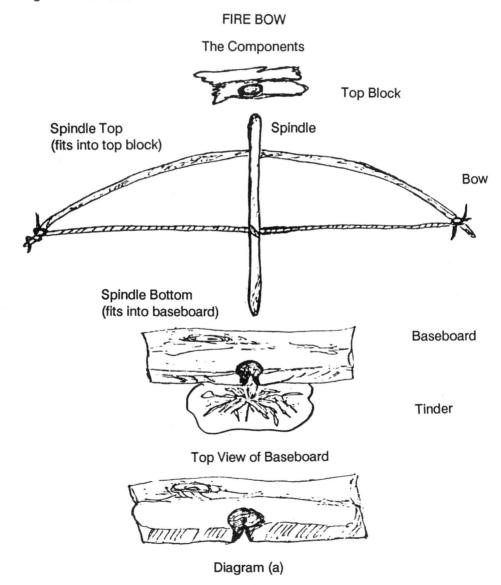

Top Block

Spindle Top
(fits into top block)

Spindle

Bow

Spindle Bottom
(fits into baseboard)

Baseboard

Tinder

Top View of Baseboard

Diagram (a)

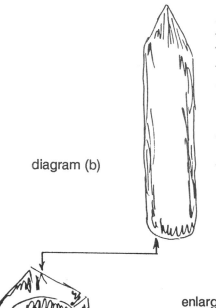

Since the top fits into a socket and must spin freely, the least amount of friction is desired. There are two recognized methods of roughing the spindle bottom to get the greatest amount of friction. The hexagon method (1) produces more friction but is more difficult to cut than the groove-drill method (2), especially if only rocks are available to make the gouges. The bottom of the spindle fits into the baseboard. We want the maximum amount of friction, thereby producing hot dust and cinder.

diagram (b)

enlarged bottom (can be more than six sides)

(1) Cross section of hexagon type roughed spindle

(2) Drill or grooved type of spindle

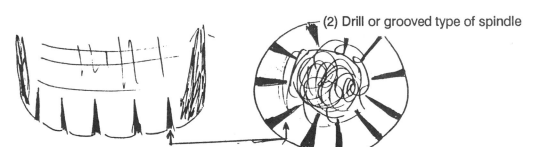

Side view of bottom.
Grooves are approximately 3 mm deep,
5 mm in length, and 1 mm wide.

diagram (c)

PREPARING THE BASEBOARD
Side view -

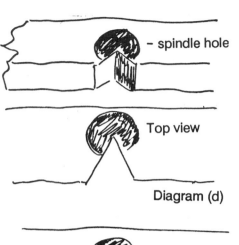

- spindle hole

Top view

Diagram (d)

diagram (e)

BASEBOARD NOTCH
- cut to centre of spindle hole.
Size of spindle hole itself depends on size of spindle's diameter; in order to function, spindle must fit snugly into hole.
If hole is too big, spindle will rotate without any resistance; hence, no friction.

The friction resulting from spinning the spindle in the baseboard causes an ultra-fine powder to accumulate or pile up in the notch area. This powder is extremely hot, and can be blown into a flame. Sometimes, it forms a red-glowing cinder. Without a properly shaped notch, such a cinder cannot form.

Tinder resting on dry piece of birch bark

When a sufficient amount of smoke has been produced (usually after 20-60 seconds), carefully remove the piece of bark with cinder or pile of hot powder, blow to a glowing redness; put into a prepared tinder nest; gently blow into a flame and transfer to a prepared pile of squawwood.

Some suggested tinder includes dry grasses, charred cloth, milkweed fluff, cattail fluff, dried juniper bark, dried and shredded cedar bark, seasoned bird nests, or a loose combination of all of these items.

NOTES

(1) Charred cloth may be used between drill and fire board to speed up the process.

(2) Woods to use: basswood, tamarack, poplar, balsam, jack pine, cedar, elm, or willow.

In order to insure a flame, hold tinder nest in front of face. Blow gently. Once ignited, place burning nest in previously prepared kindling.

Even under ideal conditions, starting fires with the firebow is extremely difficult. However, if nothing else is available the survivor should make every attempt to obtain a fire.

A small, perforated metal container is ideal for making charred cloth. Singed cotton is one of the best methods of "catching" sparks.

In deep snows, lay a foundation of criss-crossed logs at least three layers deep. Build a fire on top of this foundation.

Once a fire has been started, do not let it go out. When someone learns how to start a fire with the firebow, he appreciates and respects the difficulties, frustrations, and troubles involved; you'll never again catch such a person without matches, or a lighter.

SOME HINTS - LOCATING WOOD FOR FIREBOW

1. Locate live specimens of the following species and cut the lower dead limbs for spindles and baseboards:
Cottonwood, Aspen, Poplar
Cedar
Basswood, Linden
Maple
Willow

2. If lower branches are all live, locate any trees in the immediate vicinity which are dead; there is a good chance that they are of the same species. This is especially true near cedar and poplar stands.

3. Try any dead wood found on the ground. It must be completely dry and a moderately soft specimen; however, the spindle and baseboard should be of the same hardness; ideally, the spindle should be slightly harder, but not the reverse.

4. For the baseboard or spindle, avoid resinous (conifers) woods if at all possible. Also, avoid hard, dense woods such as Ash, Oak, or Ironwood.

5. Any live, flexible sapling will suffice for the bow itself.
Some examples- Willow
              - Poplar
              - Alder.

MAGNIFYING GLASS AND ICE

As youngsters, many individuals learned to utilize a magnifying glass to produce heat by "bending" the sun's rays and concentrating them in a small spot. In an emergency, any optical type of instrument could be used with similar results, including binocular and telescope lens.

I have heard stories about individuals who shaped clear icicles or chunks of solid ice into a magnifying lens. Apparently, this technique, for them anyways, ultimately produced fire. For me, mastering this "ice" method, has, so far, eluded me. At the moment, I'm in the process of conducting more research on this unique method of fire starting.

TRANSPORTING FIRE

Fire Bundle

In a survival situation, fire is usually a must, a top priority along with water and shelter. Fires are hard to produce when modern fire starters are not available, that is, when the survivor must use a firebow or flint; thus, when a fire is started, never, never, never let it go out, since one may not have the energy or luck to initiate another spark. One method of keeping your fire going indefinitely when on the move, or to transport it to another site or fireplace, is by using a device to carry red-hot coals: the fire bundle.

Burn hard woods to produce hot coals (coniferous wood will not produce the desired coals). Find an old rotted piece of wood, such as a decaying stump, which contains a great deal of the semi-moist, decaying wood. However, if wood is too moist, coal will go out; if too dry, it will flame up and burn, necessitating the starting of another fire to produce the desired coals.

Ideally, the perfect stump should be a manageable size, lightweight, and fairly easy to carry. Place the burning coal on one end of the stump. Fan (by blowing) the ember, causing a small flame to smoulder in the log itself. If kept out of strong winds, the embers will continue to smoulder until the whole stump burns itself out, a process which normally takes the better part of a day.

Once ignited, punkwood smoulders for hours. Carry small log to new fire site. A few strong puffs will soon produce a flame.

96

Always be ready to prepare another bundle in the event of a sudden blaze. Some prefer to have more than one active bundle in the group should one go out. This is especially true when transporting fire in the rain.

When a permanent fire is required, fan (by blowing) the ember; a flame will start almost immediately.

SUGGESTED READING:

Assiniwi, B. *Survival in the Bush*. Toronto: Copp Clark, 1972.

Fear, E. *Surviving The Unexpected Wilderness Emergency*. Tacoma: Survival Education Assn., 1972.

Ferri, G. "Some Fire-Starting Techniques". *Angler & Hunter*, June, 1986, p. 40.

Ferri, G. "Some Emergency Fire-Starting Techniques". *Angler & Hunter*, August, 1986, p. 1.

Fry, A. *Survival in the Wilderness*. Toronto: Macmillan, 1981.

Greenbank, A. *The Book of Survival*, Harper & Row, 1967.

Gzowski, P. *The Sacrament*. Toronto: McClelland & Stewart-Bantam, 1980.

Jensen, C.E. "Don't Panic," *Field & Stream*, 1963, 68 (6): 30-32, 93-97.

Nelson, R.K. *Hunters of the Northern Forest*. Chicago: U. of Chicago Press, 1973.

Roninger, L.E., Ed. *Survival*. Department of the Army Field Manual, F. 17. No. 21-76, 1958.

Rutstrum, C. *New Way in the Wilderness*. New York: Collier, 1958.

Schuh, D.R. *Modern Survival*. Edmonton: Hurtig Publishers, 1979.

Scurlock Wm., Ed. *The Book of BuckSkinning II*. Texarkana: Rebel Publishing, 1984.

Survival Training Edition AF Manual 64-3. Washington, D.C.: U.S. Gov't Printing Office.

Wilkinson, S. "Help! Survival Kit." *Flying*, 1968, 83: 45-47

CHAPTER FOUR
You think you're hungry today...wait until tomorrow.

Stephen King

ANIMALS, SNARES AND DEADFALLS

Although small game is supposedly the mainstay of the wilderness survivor, this book will deal with food sources other than birds and animals. However, some token space is provided to the so-called food mainstay of the survivor....

RABBIT

Despite their availability, the survivor should be wary of eating solely rabbit meat. Wild rabbit meat has very little fat; hence, after a few days following a steady diet of lean rabbit meat, the victim begins to weaken.

Fat is desperately needed in the system. Without it, the victim suffers from rabbit starvation - caused by consuming only lean meats of any kind. Some nutritionists believe that such a diet sets up a protein imbalance which takes the fat out of the system. As soon as the fat is depleted, the victim weakens. Furthermore, the human body requires some amount of fat to effectively consume meats. Without this fat, meat is not properly digested and processed. The meal, therefore, goes right through the digestive system, providing little nourishment to the body.

The survivor should also be aware of animal diseases. This includes tularemia, a disease which affects wild rabbits and hares. It can be contracted by humans through open cuts, scratches and sores while skinning or dressing infected animals. All wild rabbits and hares used for food should be considered as possible carriers of rabbit or deer-fly fever (Francisella tularnsis.) The disease is more common to rabbits; however, other mammals can be carriers.

Visual signs in live animals can often be detected. A rabbit that makes little or no effort to escape, is indifferent to your presence and is easily captured or killed, should be considered as diseased. An infected animal will usually have small white spots or blotches on its liver. Under normal circumstances, infected rabbits should be considered as unfit for food.

Tularemia is a treatable disease. The symptoms and signs (usually 2 to 4 days) are sudden headaches, chills, nausea, vomiting, excessive temperatures, and severe perspiration. Competent medical attention can arrest the disease and, with no other complications, a complete cure can be assured.

The mortality among untreated cases is about 6%. Death is usually caused by overwhelming infection, pneumonia, meningitis, or peritonitis. Relapses are uncommon, but occur in inadequately treated cases. One attack confers immunity if this makes you feel any better.

We have heard for years that rabbit is high on the list as a possible food source for the man lost in the bush. While not the diet that man can subsist on for long periods of time, rabbits usually are plentiful when they are found, especially in the Arctic. They can be trapped, snared or dispatched with a throwing stick. Does this mean that we must observe a "hands off" policy with all that food hopping around? Not necessarily if we observe a few of the rules of survival, food preparation and cookery.

Wild rabbits and other rodents should be handled with great caution, especially in endemic areas. Wear gloves if you have them. Be certain that you have no cuts, scratches, or open sores on your hands. Skin the rabbit carefully, being especially careful not to nick yourself with your knife. Gut the critter and examine its liver. If the white spots are in evidence on the liver, you may want to stop right there. From

Porcupines are relatively simple to catch. For this reason, they have often beeen called the survivor's "friend".

here on, it will depend on how hungry you are. If hunger is going to be your guide, discard the liver, quarter the carcass and put it in the pot to boil.

Boiling is best if you have a pot, as you will have soup and meat. Roasting on a spit is second best, but you won't have the soup. Cook thoroughly - well done - beyond questionable doubt. While all this cooking is going on, wash your hands and knife thoroughly, using plenty of water. Do not touch any part of the skin or discarded parts after washing.

FOX, WOLF AND COYOTE

Apparently, these animals are relatively easy to snare in a larger version of the simple rabbit snare; however, it has been our experience that this group of animals is difficult to trap, even by professional trappers using conventional devices.

MINK, MARTIN AND LYNX

Some survival manuals suggest simple as well as complicated snares and deadfalls to obtain these animals. Although not an impossible feat, we tend to place these species in the same category as the group above. You, in our opinion, are encouraged to seek easier prey.

Crayfish - once boiled or roasted, the entire animal is edible.

MUSKRAT AND BEAVER

Should the survivor locate their runways, a modified version of the rabbit snare could be set up (use your intellect, and practice these snares before you are faced with a survival situation). We have had moderate success in trapping these animals.

PORCUPINE

This is one animal that the survivor can actually and actively hunt down. Although not as common as we are led to believe, the porcupine is nonetheless fairly plentiful throughout our forests. Watch for trees stripped of their bark fairly high off the ground. A club is usually sufficient to kill porcupines. Commence skinning from its stomach area.

MICE, MOLES AND SHREWS

These should not be overlooked as a food source; however, do not actively hunt for them. Should they cross your path, throw them into the stew (gutted, of course).

CHIPMUNKS

These common animals are found in most wilderness areas. Snare as you would a squirrel. Throw gutted chipmunk (head included) into your stew.

Snakes are usually plentiful in most wilderness areas. They should not be overlooked as a food source.

UPLANDS GAME BIRDS AND WATERFOWL

In theory, and according to many survival texts, these are an easy prey. Some suggest the survivor hide in the reeds, covered with cattails, and pounce on the unwary birds as they swim by. Even with firearms, birds are difficult to bring down. Granted, the occasional grouse has fallen to a lucky throwing stick; actively chasing birds uses up more calories and energy than they're worth. Perhaps the survivor should concentrate on passive hunting (setting snares and deadfalls) rather than attempting to track game, a difficult act even at the best of times. Besides, making all these gadgets will keep your mind occupied, thereby keeping you from foolishly running about the forest.

Since this book is written from a practical, not a theoretical, armchair viewpoint, we hope to eliminate some myths, romantic notions, and fairy tales (there's an animal behind every tree) pertaining to wilderness survival.

Frog legs are a delicacy. Although some species such as the Pickerel frog (Rana palustris) are poisonous, most frogs are edible. Avoid toads and salamanders as a food source.

In a realistic survival situation, the victim is more likely to "hunt" for insects, eggs, snails, lizards, shellfish, leeches, and crayfish. In our opinion, the following foods are much easier to obtain in the bush:

EGGS

Collect any bird or reptile eggs. Place eggs into water; if they sink, they're edible. Roast by laying them in ashes; otherwise, boil or fry on a flat rock.

LEECHES

Sun dry until stiff and solid. They resemble and taste like unsalted anchovies.

SNAILS

Gather by any active lakeshore, forest, or field. Boil or add to your stew.

BUGS, GRUBS, AND ANTS

Can be boiled, added to stews, or roasted on a flat rock. Treat grasshoppers in a similiar fashion.

SNAKES

After skinning and gutting, chop up and add to the great stew. Should other insects venture close to your site, add them to the cooking pot. Consume everything in the pot, especially the liquid, since this fluid holds the minerals and other nutrients removed by boiling.

CRAYFISH

Spear on a sharpened stick. Roast until a bright red colour. All parts are edible.

FROGS

When catching frogs, use a flexible stick to knock them unconscious. Kill and gut the animal. Allow to dry. All parts are edible. Looks and tastes like jerky.

Don't let plate fright, that is, food that does not resemble food, scare you away; the survivor, when starving, must consume anything that will keep him alive.

A bird nest offers two things to the survivor: food and kindling material.

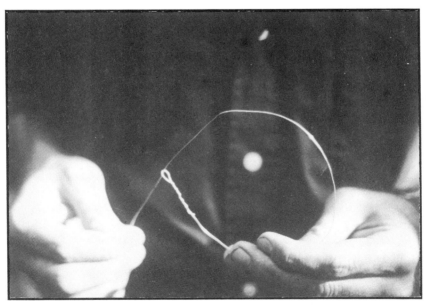

Snare loop should be free of all kinks. A freely-sliding noose will not break when closing in on an animal.

Simple Rabbit Snare

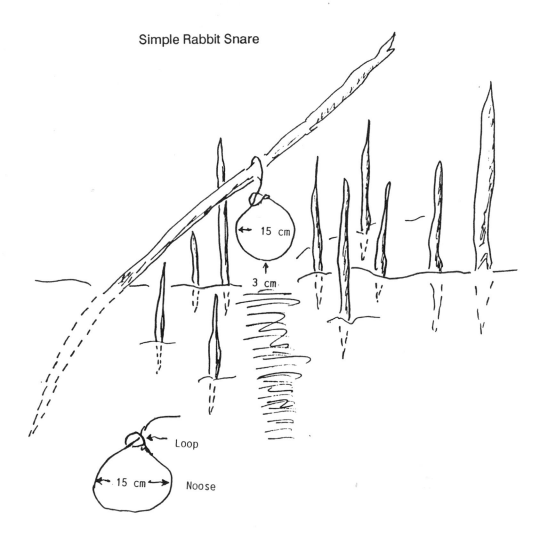

Once a runway has been found, drive a snare pole firmly into the snow near the runway. Dead sticks or boughs should be inserted into the snow to guide animals into the snare.

The survivor is advised to set up many snare poles, at various parts of the runway.

During seasons when snow is not present, the survivor can tie a snare to a tree close to the runway; however, choose a flexible sapling, since unbending trunks cause snarewire to break.

COMMON SQUIRREL SNARE

Relatively plentiful throughout Canada, squirrels offer the wilderness survivor some hope of procuring fresh meat. Since these animals are creatures of habit which often use shortcuts, this leaning pole snare is a fairly simple and effective method of catching them.

Lean a pole against a tree housing a nest or food cache. Squirrels, attempting to climb up the pole will become snared.

The survivor is well advised to set up numerous poles over a large area.

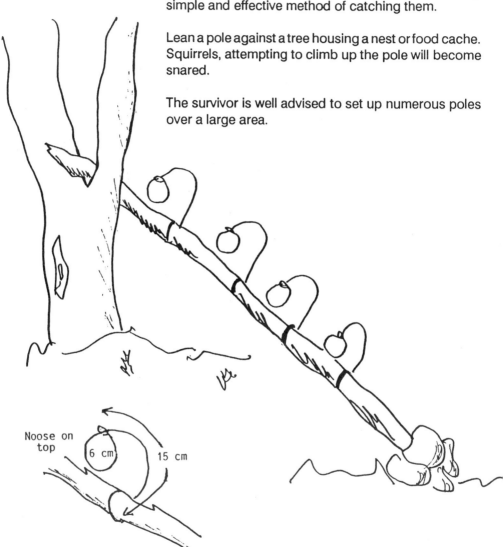

Noose on top

6 cm   15 cm

A well-placed snare is bound to produce some game. The survivor must set dozens of such snares along animal runways.

All parts of the gutted animal, including head and legs are edible.

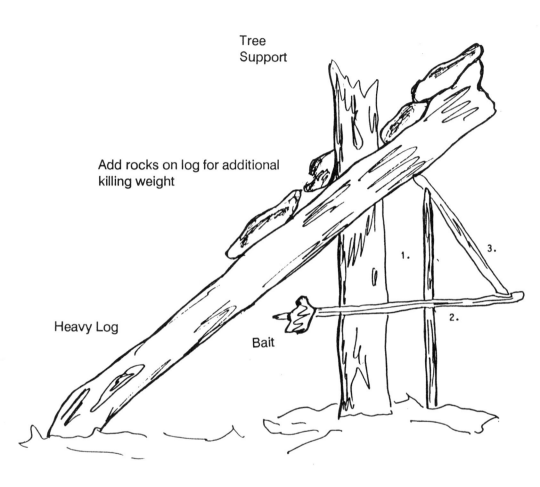

Tree
Support

Add rocks on log for additional
killing weight

Heavy Log

Bait

1.

2.

3.

FIGURE 4 DEADFALL

Constructing such devices may serve another more useful function: keeping the
survivor close to his shelter, thereby preventing him from aimlessly wandering
through the wilderness.

108

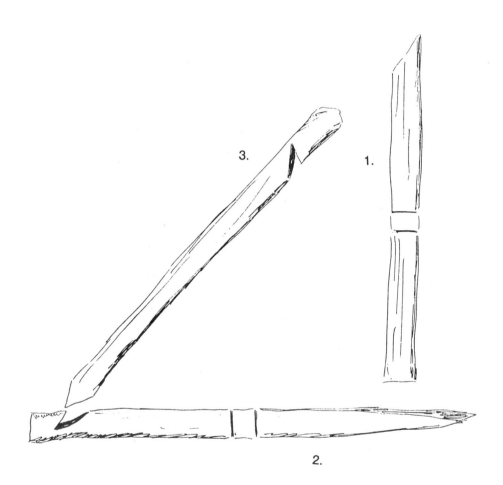

SINGLE SUPPORT (SIMPLE) DEADFALL

Tree Support

Notch

Rocks

Heavy Log

Bait

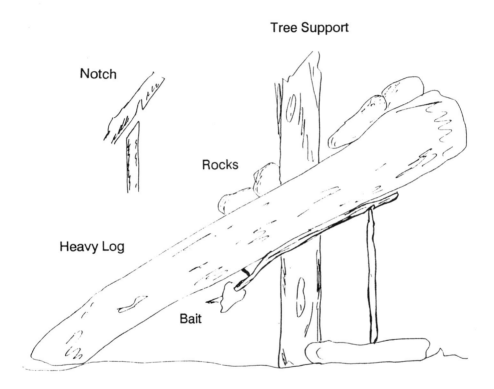

Figure 4 deadfalls may occasionally trap an animal. In our opinion, however, this deadfall serves another purpose: keeping the victim's mind occupied, thereby preventing him from wandering through the wilderness.

Since these readily available food sources are not to be had during the winter months, the survivor is advised to remain relatively close to his shelter and consume copious amounts of teas and hot liquids.

SOME EMERGENCY GEAR: FISHING

FISH HOOKS

In order to acquire fish to survive, a simple fish hook can be devised using either wood or bone. Wood is easier material to work with and easier to come by. Whittle a sliver of wood approximately 1 cm wide and 4 cm in length, with both ends sharpened to a point. Make one half of the hook thicker. This will ensure that the heavier end points down, thus enabling a fish to swallow it easier. Notch the middle, tying a string to the hook.

The fish hook can then be baited using grubs, maggots, insects or, if available, rotting flesh. If bone is available, use it! Instead of whittling, use stones to sand down a sliver of bone to the approximate size of the fish hook.

For string, use bootlaces or unravel yarn from sweater.

Admittedly, these hooks rarely work, even under the best of circumstances. Making them, however, keeps the lost victim close to his shelter. Furthermore, the survivor's mind is actively involved in making an item which might supply him with some food. These hooks enable the victim to keep his wits in order by forestalling boredom.

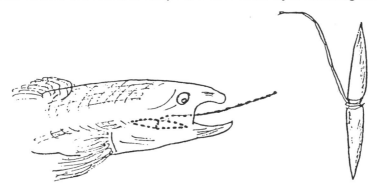

HARPOON

An ancient device used by Canada's Native People, the simple harpoon can be fashioned from wood or bone. Harpoons have three parts: point, shaft and string.

The harpoon is approximately 5 cm long, 3 cm wide and 5 mm in thickness. Use hardwoods to ensure strength if bone is unavailable. First, whittle the wood into the above proportions, later carving the barbs (this keeps the fish from slipping off the harpoon) and a point at one end. The last step in making the harpoon is to drill a hole at the end. Use your knife point.

Cut a sapling approximately 2 meters in length, splitting one end of the pole and wedging the harpoon into this split.

Finally, lash the harpoon onto the shaft. A 40 cm piece of string is tied to the blade and to the shaft. When a fish is struck, it is secured to the pole.

Spruce root that has been soaked and split makes excellent string.

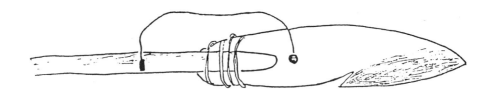

Splitting wood to fashion harpoons.

Complete bone knife and harpoon point. Making such devices keeps the lost victim close to his shelter. By performing this task, the survivor's mind, being active, does not succumb to boredom.

A simple device, this throwing stick can be hurled at small game or used to dig out roots and tubers.

Flat rock used as frying pan.

COOKING MEAT AND FISH

Boiling is the best method of preparing meat for human consumption since it is easy and requires less fuel than other methods. If you drink the resulting broth, you are getting the full food value. In order to ensure that all meat is cooked, cut all the chunks of meat the same size.

Frying can be done if utensils, such as flat rock or skillet, are available, and if there is sufficient food. Remember that some of the food value is wasted, and above the tree line there will be a very limited supply of fuel.

Barbecuing or roasting is an easy method and often produces the tastiest results. It does, however, cause the most waste. After cleaning the fish or small animal, spike it onto the end of a stick elevated beside a hot fire. Use a green stick and try to build a fire which produces little flame. Turn the meat regularly to ensure it is thoroughly cooked. A great quantity of nutritious liquid is lost by this method and there is considerable shrinkage. This can be partially countered by placing the meat very close to the fire at first to form a crust on the outside, or hang the meat at one end of the fire with a shallow plate or tin underneath to catch the drippings.

BAKED EGGS:

Wrap each egg in a few layers of wet leaves and leave to cook in hot coals/ ashes for approximately 20 minutes.

Hot coals or embers should be used when cooking meats. Open flames merely burn, not cook, the food.

This is one of the simplest methods of suspending a pot over the fire. While one end holds the pot, the other end is embedded into the ground (or snow).

Cooking fish or meat on a split log.

Butt end of pole is held in place by forked stick embedded into ground. The pole can be rotated to roast all sides of the meat. A container under the meat catches all drippings.

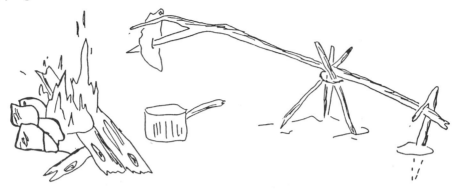

Fires built in open areas merely create drafts. Fires with stone reflectors not only channel heat towards the survivor, they radiate a greater amount of heat. As the rock warms up, it also becomes a substantial heat source.

STEAM COOKER PIT

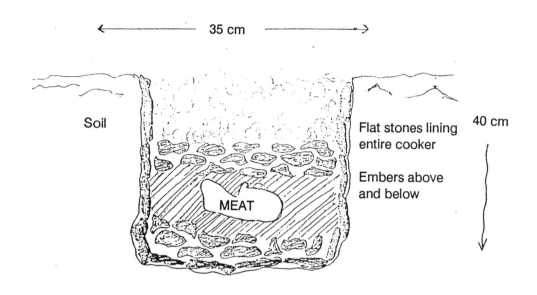

Dig a hole approximately 40 cm deep and 35 cm wide. Line sides and bottom with flat, dry, granite rocks.

Burn hardwoods, until 10 cm of charcoal has accumulated at the bottom. Place meats (or bannock) encased in greens onto charcoal bed.

Add foliage plants (another 10 cm) on top of coals and meats.

Burn additional hardwoods over plants, forming another layer of coals.

Cover entire pit with dirt. Leave for approximately 60 to 90 minutes, depending on size of item to be cooked.

Do not bother to pluck the feathers from a gutted bird. Cover the entire bird with a coating of clay approximately 1 cm thick. Same principle can be used to cook fish. Clay will soon harden. When broken, feathers or scales will come off with the clay.

FRYING PAN BAKING

BANNOCK

Bannock is made by simply adding berries (dried raisins are ideal) to a hardtack (flour and water) mixture. Make patties approximately one centimetre thick. Bake like hardtack. If frying pan is not available, wrap dough around a green stick and place near fire. Turn occasionally. Bake until golden brown.

STONE FRYING PAN

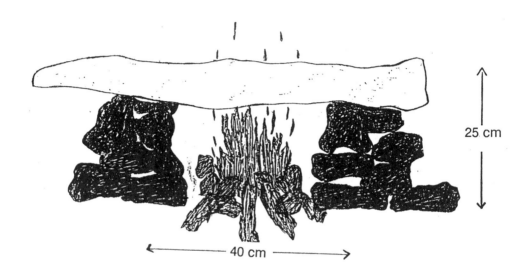

Place any flat, dry, granite rock over flame, and support with two walls. Leave ends completely open for better ventilation.

Wet or damp rocks tend to crack easily, or sometimes explode.

Limestone should not be used - it explodes when heated!

Once a flat stone has been thoroughly heated, use like a frying pan. Also, the "frying pan" acts as an umbrella, keeping raindrops away from burning embers.

Do not waste time constructing a wood reflector. Too much time and effort is required. Instead, utilize a suitable rock.

COOKING WITH GREENS:

Wrap meat/vegetables in large green leaves, making certain the leaves are tightly sealed but loosely fitted around the food. Throw into embers; wait until the fire has burned down to hot coals with very little blaze. Leave for approximately 30 to 60 minutes.

JERKY AND PEMMICAN

These two foods, created by Natives and Frontiersmen, make ideal survival meals.

From earliest times, primitive people solved the problem of preserving meat by cutting it into strips and drying it. Later, colonists and frontiersmen moving westward, learned from Natives how to dry meats, used this food as standard fare. It is nourishing, tastes good, could be chewed while walking or riding, and requires no cooking fire.

Although the Natives used mostly deer and buffalo, beef jerky sustained many a cowboy and was a survival item in many saddlebags. Anyone can easily and economically make his own jerky. Any lean meat can be used.

JERKY (KITCHEN VARIETY)

Lean Meat - Seasoning

Trim all the fat from the meat. Cut into strips measuring two to three cm wide, three mm thick, and twenty to thirty cm long. Place a layer of the strips over an open rack, evenly spacing the strips. Put the rack into an oven no warmer than 150 degrees. Leave door slightly open. Bake until the meat is completely dry, about eight hours, but longer if necessary. The idea is to dehydrate meat thoroughly, not to cook it.

In the comfort of your kitchen, you can vary seasonings with herb salts, such as celery, onion, or garlic. Add a bit of Tobasco, or sprinkle the finished strips with A-1 Sauce. For an extra salty taste, before beginning the process pickle the meat strips in heavy brine for a few hours and then rinse them off.

Try inventing a marinade of your own, soaking the strips overnight before placing in an oven. You don't need to refrigerate the jerky but you must keep it dry. Mold can be wiped off, but if the sticks become limp from dampness, they will spoil. Airtight cans are good for storage.

SMOKED JERKY

Lean Meat - Smoke

After cutting meat into proper sized strips, dip a few of the strips at a time into a pot of continuously boiling water. Remove when the outside turns whitish, and thoroughly drain the strips. If pots are unavailable, dry strips in direct sunlight until they harden. Hang strips on a green stick and put over smoky, punky fire. The length of smoking time varies, usually 5-10 hours. The thicker the jerky strips, the longer the process. The smoking rack housing the jerky should be completely covered, if all possible. The smoke serves to discourage insects. It also gives the meat a more pleasant flavour.

The thick strips are softer inside than the thin ones, and look somewhat like smoked ham. Unrefrigerated, they do not keep as long, but they can be frozen. Sliced into thin shavings, these thick strips can be thrown into a stew or eaten as is.

PEMMICAN

Pemmican is an all meat product. It is the most compact, nutritious, complete single food known to man. Many consider it to be the most satisfying, all weather ration for survival or trail operations.

The origin of pemmican dates back some 400 years to the American Plains Indian. It is credited with carrying the early explorers across the continent, sustaining the fur trade, carrying Robert Peary to the North Pole and Ronald Amundsen to the South Pole. Vilhjalmur Stefansson, considered to be one of the greatest of Arctic explorers, praised pemmican as the most valuable for all concentrated foods. Stefansson did not limit its use to the Arctic or to winter. His recommendations were for all zones and seasons. In recent times, it has been the mainstay and emergency ration for polar expeditions.

No other food has had the credit and discredit of pemmican. The discredit has come from adulteration. The white man added berries, cereals, dried fruit and anything else that was edible and handy. It is true that these additions varied or changed the flavour; however, by adding other ingredients, pemmican has ceased to have the nutritional value for its weight and it no longer has the advantage over other trail foods. For example, it takes about 60 grams of dried fruit to make up the food value in approximately 30 grams of true pemmican.

Pemmican was never intended to be a delicacy or confection. It was, and still is, considered to be a "stay alive" food. The other advantages of this time tested ration is that it may be eaten cooked or uncooked, seasoned or unseasoned, and it has excellent keeping qualities in all climates. Robert Scott's cache of pemmican left in the Antarctic over seventy years ago was found to be still edible by the expedition that visited his camp.

MAKING PEMMICAN

First you make jerky. "Jerking" will reduce three kilograms of lean beef or venison to one kilogram of dried meat. Cut the meat into 1 cm strips (the thinner, the more quickly dried) and clean it of all fat. The primitives dried the meat in the sun or by smoking. Smoking keeps the insects off and gives meat a smoke flavour. Use only wood from broad leaf trees. Do not use the leaves or the wood or needles of evergreens. Maple, alder or willow wood is good. Don't produce too much heat-you're smoking, not cooking. Jerky can also be made in an oven at the lowest possible heat setting. With a gas oven the pilot light is sufficient. Leave the oven door open slightly so moisture from the meat can escape.

Drying will take from 10 to 15 hours. When a strip of meat breaks when bent, it is dry. Pulverize the meat by pounding with stone. Place a cup full of the meat in a bowl. With this, mix the grease rendered from beef suet. Beef kidney suet is considered the best.

Render the suet in a frying pan over a very low heat. When the suet will give no more grease, pour an approximate weight of grease equal to the weight of pulverized meat into the bowl and stir so that the grease mixes thoroughly with the meat. But only use the liquid grease; no pieces of suet. Strangely, fat left on meat made into jerky ruins the meat, but pure fat rendered into grease preserves pemmican.

The 50/50 mix may be too rich for the beginning pemmican eater, so you may wish to mix the first small batch with two-thirds meat to one-third fat. Whatever your mix, do not add seasoning, nuts, berries, dry fruit or anything else. Mixing other ingredients at this time will tend to reduce the storage life. Seasoning and other additives can be mixed in just before eating.

RECIPES

As is...pemmican can be eaten cold and without cooking. It is not as palatable and will stick to the roof of the mouth like peanut butter. Cooked or cold, it's still a good stay-alive food.

"Browned pemmican"...Crumble the pemmican in a pan and cover with water. Add salt and other seasoning. Allow to stand for at least 10 minutes until meat has absorbed enough water to become soft. Stir to keep the meat from burning.

"Meat gruel"...Crumble the pemmican in a pan. Add sufficient water to make a thick soup. Add salt and other seasoning. Allow to stand 5 to 10 minutes, then heat with occasional stirring.

The taste of pemmican improves with hunger. The hungrier you are, the better it tastes. Prepared and sealed as described, pemmican will be edible for several years. When not being carried, it should be stored in a cool, dry place. A batch of approximately 120 grams is about all you can consume in one day. Pemmican is a thirst creator so it is advisable to have plenty of water available when eating it in any form.

GUT TWINE

Since the survivor must develop a no-waste attitude, he is encouraged to utilize all parts of a snared or trapped animal. Besides consuming the flesh, a victim can use bones to fashion hooks; intestines become bait; hides are always needed for extra garments; while other internal organs provide the wilderness survivor with twine.

Cat gut! Everyone's heard of tennis racquets strung with cat gut, or cat gut fishing line. Most people use the phrase "Cat Gut" without really thinking of what it is.

A very good use for the intestines of animals is to make it into a string-like material. A good way to get some practice, before trying it with animals caught in the field, is

Stretched and dried animal hides ready for smoke tanning.

SMOKE TANNING

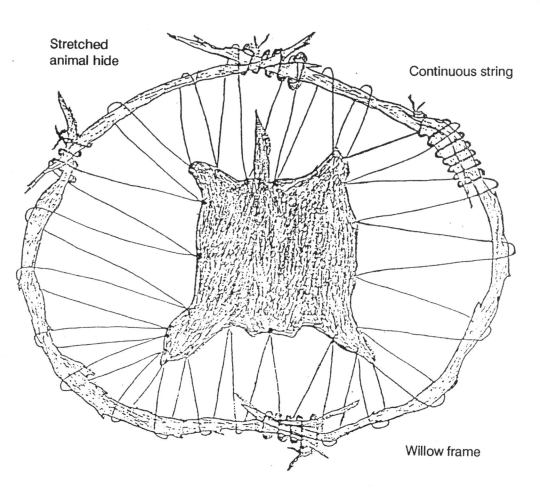

Stretched animal hide

Continuous string

Willow frame

Scrape hide clean of all flesh and fat, then dry skin in direct sunlight for one full day.

Stretch hide tightly over willow frame using one continuous strand of string if at all possible.

Place over punkwood fire for at least one day.

Cover entire structure with boughs or tarp to trap smoke.

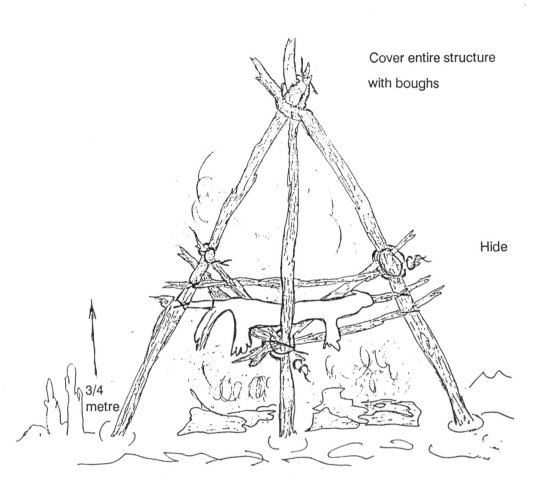

Cover entire structure with boughs

Hide

3/4 metre

Once the tripod has been erected, start a fire. Cover flames with punkwood (rotting wood) to create plenty of smoke but no flame. Beware of a sudden breeze. This will cause a flame, causing everything to burn. Cover entire structure with boughs or tarp, leaving only a small opening to add punkwood, as required. Allow to smoke for 6 to 12 hours, depending on thickness of hide.

When smoke tanning, great care must be taken not to "cook" the hide. Once the flame is produced, cover open fire with punkwood. The resulting billows of smoke will tan the skin. Cover the entire structure with boughs. Beware of sudden breezes - they'll fan the flames.

to obtain some hog gut, commonly called sausage casing. Try your local butcher, who makes his own sausage, or a butcher supply company. Get the real intestine, not synthetic casing. It usually comes moist and salted. This way, it will keep for quite a long time in the refrigerator.

To use it, first rinse in water. Next, tie one end to a fence or door knob or branch. Stretch the gut out, expressing as much water as you can, twisting until good and tight and well twined. We usually twist the gut until it begins to double twist. Later, secure the end to a twig and stake it in the ground until completely dry (usually about a day). When dry, coil and save it for future use.

Use this gut anywhere you would use thread, string, etc. Experiment: Try twisting two or three strands for increased strength; try braiding the dried material.

SMOKE TANNING

Scrape hide clean of all flesh and fat, then dry skin in direct sunlight for one full day. Stretch hide tightly over willow frame using one continuous strand of string if at all possible. Rub the animal's brain into the stretched hide.
Place over punkwood fire for at least one full day.

Once the tripod has been erected, start a fire. Cover flames with punkwood (rotting wood) to create plenty of smoke but no flame. Beware of a sudden breeze. This will cause a flame, causing everything to burn. Cover entire structure with boughs or tarp, leaving only a small opening to add punkwood, as required. Allow to smoke for 6 - 12 hours, depending on thickness of hide.

When hide is a golden-brown colour, it's tanned.

SPRUCE ROOTS

One of nature's finest materials for sewing bark objects is the tough, thin root of Black Spruce or Jack Pine. A good place to gather them is along areas exposed by erosion. Sometimes, they can be found directly under the tree, growing close to the surface. They are also very common in spruce bogs, growing in large (and long) numbers immediately below the ground. One simply pulls the root from the soil and follows along until it breaks or disappears under larger roots. Ideally, the thickness should be no greater than a pencil.

Soak the roots in water for at least two days. Remove the bark. If root is too thick, split in half. Thicker roots can be split until the desired thickness is obtained.

Properly folded sheets of birch bark make waterproof drinking and cooking utensils.

ADDITIONAL SKILLS

THE SIMPLE BIRCH BARK CUP

(1.) Remove from tree with knife (approx. 20 cm x 40 cm)
     Choose samples free of "dark" staining. Soak in water overnight.

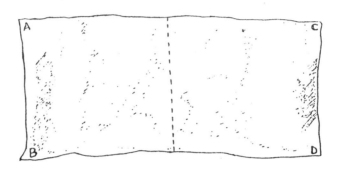

(2.)   Fold in half. Do not allow bark to tear at the folds.

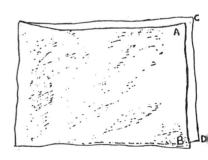

Fold sample again. You have effectively folded original sheet into quarters. Water will stay in fold BD and CA.

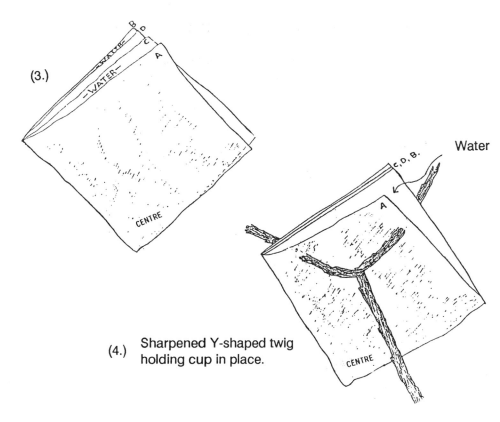

(3.)

Water

(4.) Sharpened Y-shaped twig holding cup in place.

SEAMLESS BARK PAN

Once the birch bark has been soaking in water for at least two days, fold the edges or corners in a V-angle. The result will be a seamless, waterproof container. Fasten ends with spruce roots or a pin of wood.

Such containers can be used for cooking by dropping hot stones in a dishful of water until meal is cooked.

A great deal of skill and patience is required when working with Birch bark and Spruce roots. Not only are these items, especially Spruce roots, difficult to obtain due to the bugs inhabiting Spruce bogs, they frequently break, crack, or split even under the most ideal conditions. Making these containers will not be an easy task for the novice. But if no other container is available, patience, perseverance, and desperation must prevail. As we have often stated, an emergency situation is not the time to test your expertise...practice making bark containers under controlled conditions until this skill becomes second nature.

ONE PIECE BARK CONTAINER

A. Birch piece, after soaking for two days. Soak spruce root along with bark.

B. Fold in corners. Bind ends with split and peeled spruce root.

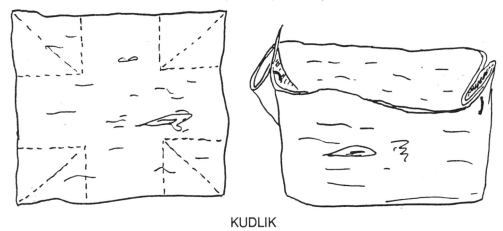

KUDLIK

The Inuit had a unique method of providing light and heat, a method which can be adapted to survival situations when needed. The materials needed to create a basic Kudlik are fuel, wick and pan.

The pan can be made from any flat shallow dish, usually found in a backpacker's knapsack. The wick, from gauze found in any first Aid Kit or from cloth. Even dried moss will do. Fuel can be melted fat or petroleum jelly.

The wick should be thoroughly saturated in the fuel. Hang a few centimeters of wick out of the pan. Coil the rest in the container. The remainder of the fuel can be added into the pan as it continues to burn.

SIDE PROFILE OF KUDLIK

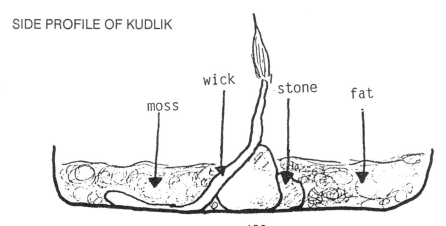

SUGGESTED READING

Auel, J. M. *The Clan of the Cave Bear*. Toronto: Bantam Books, 1980.

Berglund, B. *The Complete Wilderness Almanac*. Toronto: Pagurian Press, 1973.

Bird, R. *Alone*. Putnam, 1938.

Ferri, G. F. *Wilderness Survival*. Toronto: Humber Press, 1980.

Graves, R. H. *Food and Water in the Bush - How to Live off the Land*. J. M. Graves, 1952.

Harding, A. R. *Deadfalls and Snares*. Columbus: A. R. Harding, 1935.

Jaegar, E. *Tracks and Trailcraft*. MacMillan, 1948.

Merrill, W. *The Survival Handbook*. New York: Winchester Press, 1976.

Ormond, C. *Complete Book of Outdoor Lore*. Harper & Row, 1964.

Starnes, R. "Think...and Live." *Field and Stream,* 1963, 68 (6): 12 - 15, 112, 135.

Thompson, R. *Traps and Snares*. Lynnwood: Ray Thompson Co.

Wheat, M. M. *Survival Skills of the Primitive Paiutes*. Reno: University of Nevada Press.

CHAPTER 5
Adopt the pace of nature; her secret is patience.

--Emerson.

POISONOUS PLANTS

With the number of edible plants available to the survivor, why bother learning to identify some poisonous plants? Simply put -- so that he doesn't inadvertently harm himself! As an example, being able to identify poison ivy will ensure one's comfort in the bush by not getting a potentially dangerous rash.

When dealing with dangerous plants, the resulting sickness could tip the scales against you in a survival situation. It must be stressed that there are no rules governing what to eat. Birds can eat berries that are poisonous to humans, and bears can eat Henbane or Dolls-eyes without any ill effects; however, these same plants could kill the person who eats them. Don't be the one who mistakenly believes that humans can eat whatever animals eat.

Knowing a plant is the only means of identifying a potentially useful or harmful plant. An example which comes to mind is Wild Carrot or Queen Anne's Lace (*Daucus carota*) --a delicious and nutrious plant. To the novice, it resembes Water Hemlock (*Cicuta maculata*), one of this continent's most deadly plants. Some recommend not bothering with either plant; we, however, suggest that the student familiarize himself thoroughly with all edible and poisonous plants and be able to differentiate the two categories.

Edible plants could supply the survivor with a steady supply of food, if he knows what and where to harvest.

POISON IVY *(Rhus radicans)*

Another aspect of encountering potentially poisonous plants is via preparation. Acorns, the poisonous nut of the Oak tree (*Quercus* spp.), if boiled repeatedly or buried for a few days to leach out the tannic acid, can be eaten. There are other plants, although poisonous, which can be made edible by use of certain cooking techniques. Again, to do this safely, understand which plants can be effectively prepared. Mayapple is listed as a poisonous plant, and, in fact, all parts of this plant are poisonous, including the fruit; and yet, when the fruit is ripe (to the point of falling off the plant), it can be safely eaten. Study those plants which could be a possible food source at different times of the year.

North of the tree line, don't worry about poisonous plants, but south of the tree line, there are three which you should be aware of since they seem to cause most of the recorded problems.

The Death Cap (*Amanita* spp.) mushroom is one that hurts many people. Although it is reasonably easy to distinguish as a poisonous mushroom when mature, the young Death Cap mushroom is indistinguishable from edible varieties. This is why it is important to avoid mushrooms in the button stage. In maturity, the Death Cap has a cup-like formation at the base and a broad collar-like ring part way up the stem.

Water Hemlock (Cicuta maculata) - one of the most poisonous plants in North America.

As previously mentioned, Water Hemlock (*Cicuta maculata*) is another plant that causes problems. This is probably because it is easily confused with Cow Parsnip, an edible plant. Twenty to one hundred and twenty cm tall, it is considered to be the most poisonous plant in North America; the roots which are hollow tubes emit a parsnip odor. It is a member of the carrot family; learn to recognize it.

Baneberries (*Actaea* spp.) are another dangerous species. Approximately half a metre tall, these plants develop small white flowers which are later replaced by red or white berries. The flowers grow in short thick terminal clusters; the root stalk is quite substantial. These terminal clusters of berries are quite characteristic of this plant. All parts are toxic.

Knowing the poisonous plants commonly found in the wilds is a fascinating part of the study of wilderness survival. Taking the time to understand them, can, one day, save your life!

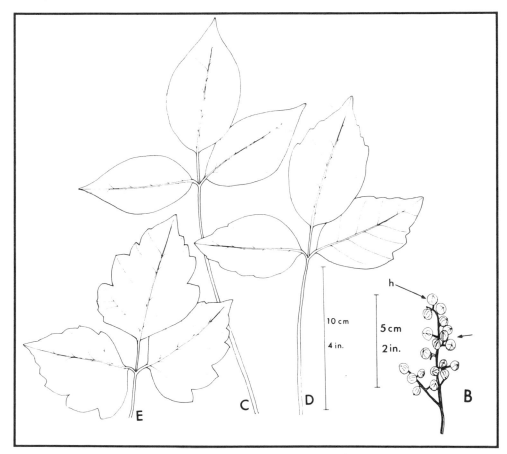

Poison Ivy. A. Low-growing form with short erect stem and a flower cluster from the axil of one compound leaf. B. Cluster of dry, white, berry-like fruits produced from the flower cluster. C - E. Variation in margin and lobing of leaflets.

137

SUMMARY: SOME POISONOUS OR DANGEROUS PLANTS

NAME	PARTS	SYMPTOM	LOCATION
Poison Ivy (*Rhus radicans*)	Whole plant	Rash	Field, Woods
Oaks (Acorns)*(*Quercus* spp.)	Raw acorns	Stomach cramps	Wooded
Buttercup (*Ranunculus acris*)	Flower	Cramps, vomiting	Field
Jack in the Pulpit* (*Arisaema atorubens*)	Raw root	Burning taste	Wooded
Common Nightshade (*Solanum nigrum*)	Berries	Cramps	Field
Baneberries (*Actaea* spp.)	Berry	Cramps	Wooded
Buckthorns (*Rhumnus* spp.)	Leaves, fruit	Cramps, vomiting	Field
Mayapple* (*Podophyllum peltatum*)	Whole plant, Unripened fruit	Cramps	Wooded
Ground Cherry* (*Physalis* spp.)	Whole plant, Unripened berry	Cramps	Field
Pokeweed* (*Phytolacca americana*)	Mature plant	Vomiting	Field
Water Hemlock (*Cicuta maculata*)	Whole plant	Vomiting, death	Aquatic
Poison Oak (*Rhus toxicodendron*)	Whole plant	Rash	Wooded

SOME POISONOUS OR DANGEROUS PLANTS CONT'D

Poison Sumac (*Rhus vernix*)	Whole plant	Rash	Wooded, wet areas
False Hellebore (*Veratum viride*)	Whole plant	Diarrhea	Wooded, swamps
Dogbanes (*Apocynum* spp.)	Juice-stem	Cramps	Wet areas
Monkshood (*Aconitum uncinatum*)	Whole plant	Vomiting	Damp slopes
Lupines (*Lupinus perennis*)	Seeds	Toxic	Field/Open Woods
Spring Larkspur (*Delphinium tricorne*)	Whole plant	Convulsions	Wooded
Wild Iris (*Iris* spp.)	Roots	Vomiting	Marshes
Canada Moonseed (*Minispermum canadense*)	Seeds	Cramps	Moist woods
Jimsonweed (*Datura stramonium*)	Whole plant	Hallucinations	Field

* EDIBLE ONLY IF PROPERLY PREPARED

MAYAPPLE *(Podophyllum peltatum)*

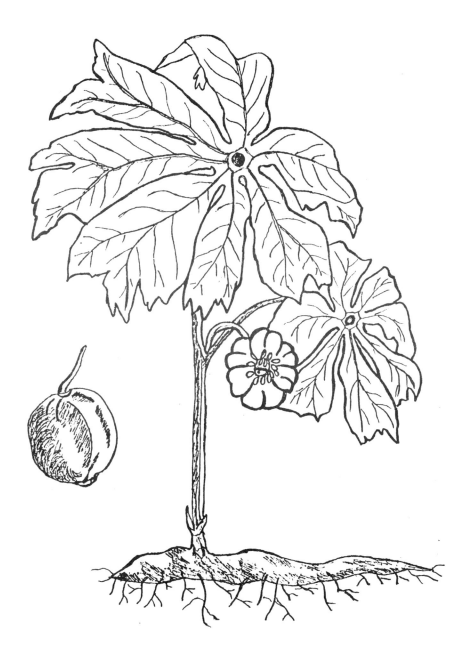

SOME COMMON EDIBLE PLANTS: AN INTRODUCTION

It is not the intent of this unit to list all edible plants found coast to coast, or to turn the reader into an instant expert on edible plants. Instead, this section merely serves to introduce the reader to a very small sampling of the edible wild.

When dealing with these plants, be prepared to divide this list into two main categories:

     i) "wants-to" plants, and
     ii) "gots-to" plants

The first group accommodates those luscious goodies we tend to harvest periodically. They taste good! Plants on this list include Fiddleheads, Leeks, Blueberries, and Raspberries. However, the wilderness survivor frequently must resort to foraging for plants having a strong or bitter taste. Simply put, it's either consume this type of plant, or quite possibly, perish. This is the "gots-to" group, which includes Pine trees (*Pinus* spp.), Burdock (*Arctium* spp.), Slippery Elm (*Ulmus rubra*), and Rock Tripe (*Umbilicaria* spp.)

We cannot over-emphasize, however, that the survivor be completely familiar with the edible, useful, and poisonous wild, as well as with their location. This could mean the difference between life and death!

With regard to foraging, the survivor must always weigh the pros and cons of harvesting plants: the energy required for this work against the energy derived from the collected food. In other words, are <u>more</u> calories being spent harvesting, than received when eating the plants? Personally, I would not range too far from my

Red Baneberry (Actaea rubra) - if consumed, fruit causes severe cramps.

141

LABRADOR TEA *(Ledum groenlandicum)*

Labrador tea is located in moist areas such as bogs, swamps, marshes and muskeg. Available year round, the leaves may be boiled to produce a tea.

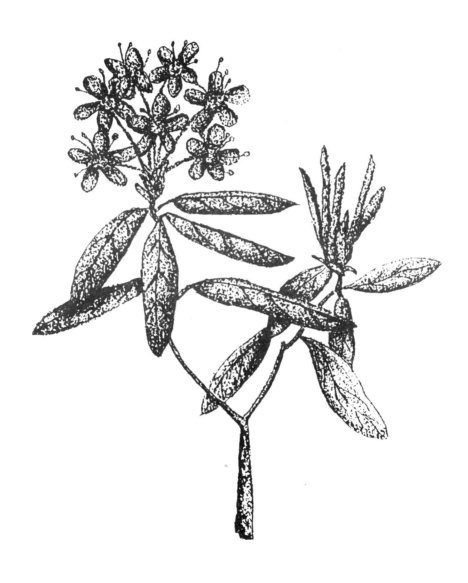

WILD CARROT *(Daucus carota)*

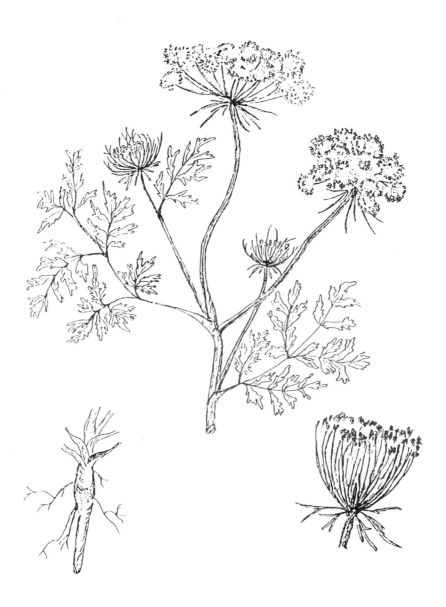

YARROW *(Achillea millefolium)*

PLANTAIN (*Plantago major*)

This prolific weed grows everywhere, especially in open fields. Although the young shoots are, by far, the tastiest part of the plant (boiled or eaten raw), the leaves can be consumed during the spring, summer and early fall. Seeds are ground and made into flour. Other uses include crushing the leaves and roots to make a green dye. Also called Ribwort and Soldiers' Herb, crushed Plantain is an antiseptic, and therefore very useful for cuts and bug bites.

BULL THISTLE *(Cirsium vulgare)*

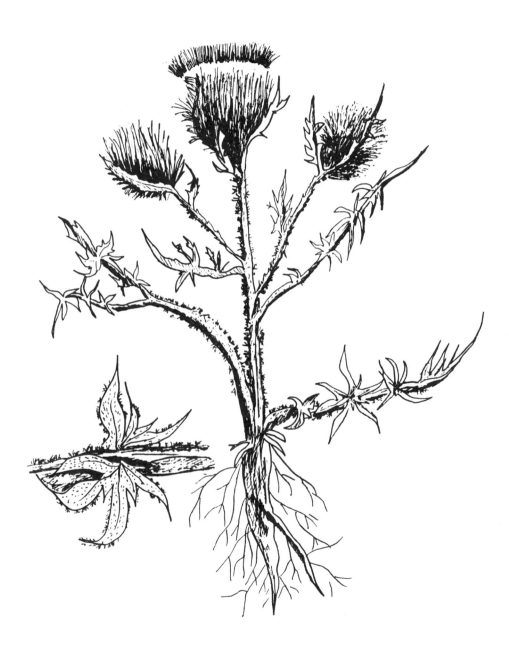

MILKWEED *(Asclepias syriaca)*

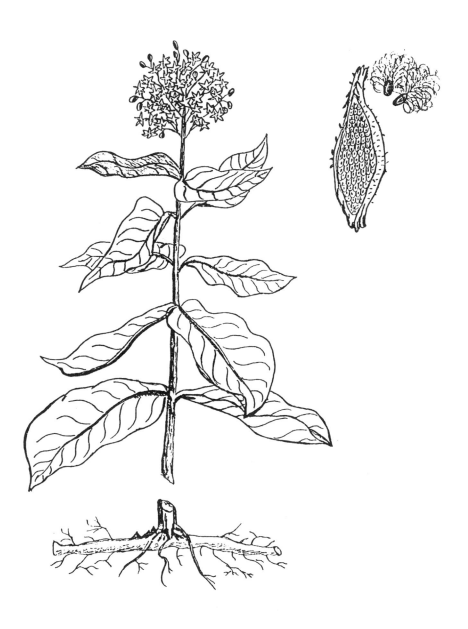

JACK-IN-THE-PULPIT (*Arisaema atrorubens*)

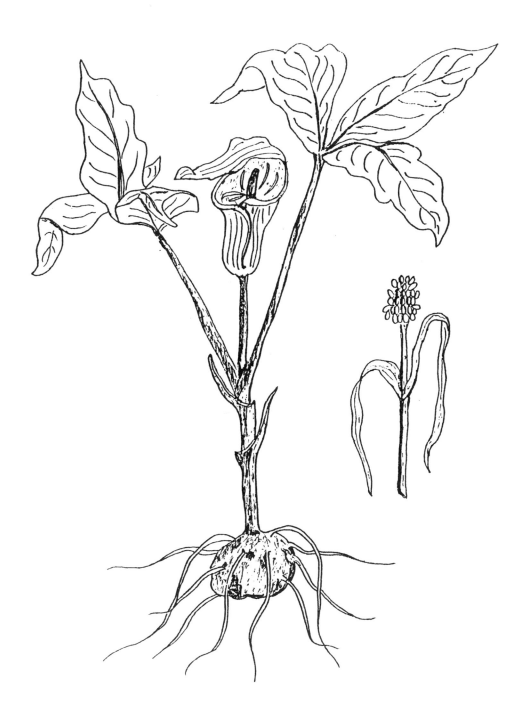

ROCK TRIPE (*Umbilicaria* spp.)

Rock Tripe resembles leaves adhering to rocks, crisp when dry, and limp, leathery when wet; colour of upper surface is gray to black. Plant contains abundant starch, and, when boiled yields a jelly-like mange containing a bitter purgative content. This can be removed by boiling and discarding the first water.

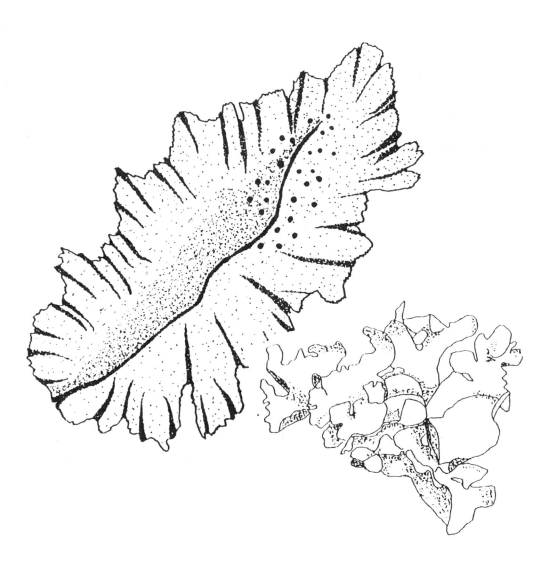

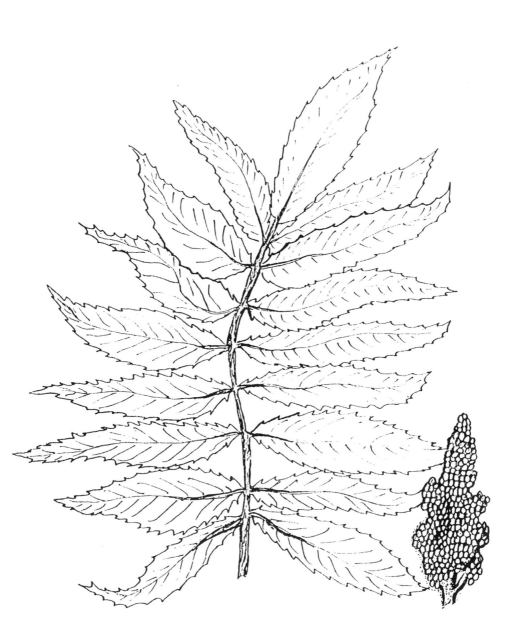

shelter simply because the nutrients gained would probably not compensate the energy expended in their collection unless, of course, an area was extremely productive.

Food, it seems, is near the bottom of the victim's priority list. Having made this statement, I must admit that there are times when a plant's nutrient or psychological values justify collection. If the survivor is stranded close to a Raspberry (*Rubus* spp.) patch, in an oak grove, or close to an abundance of cattails, the energies spent on their procurement will undoubtedly be balanced by their consumption. On other occasions, one may need to forage for psychological reasons, even if calories are wasted.

We have experienced and seen the tremendous boost the survivor receives when masticating anything that remotely resembles food.

During the winter months the choice of plants is extremely limited. Bitterly cold conditions are a constant hazard, while snow obscures much of the ground vegetation and restricts movement. Some of the plants we've listed may be visible above the snow, and usually occur in recognizable land features. Based on survival training, it becomes a matter of fine judgement whether the effort to harvest is worthwhile.

We cannot over-emphasize, however, that a complete familiarization with the edible wild, as well as its location, could mean the difference between life and death. Also, some may recognize a plant when in flower; and yet, these individuals may not be

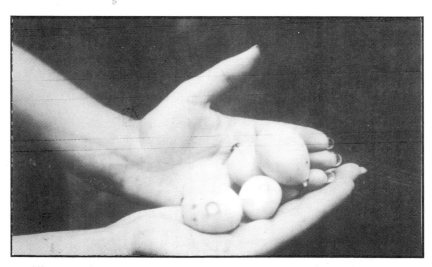

All parts of the Mayapple (Podophyllum peltatum) are poisonous, including its unripened fruit. When fully ripe, the "apples" are quite tasty.

able to recognize it, fruiting, when hungry. One book I thoroughly recommend is *A Field Guide to Edible Wild Plants* by L. Peterson. It makes an effort to portray plants throughout the seasons <u>and</u> lists the many ways in which to prepare them.

PARTS AND PIECES

Generally speaking, the flowering tops of most Canadian plants are safe to eat. Starch and protein are provided by the roots of many plants, including Cattails (*Typha* spp.), Wild Carrot (*Daucus carota*), and Cow-Parsnip (*Heracleum maximum*). The leaves and stems of many plants provide the necessary roughage and vitamins required to balance this diet. Either raw or boiled, these are both necessary; however, many of the vitamins are lost in the boiling process. Such plants include Cattail, Fiddleheads (*Pteretis pensylvanica*), Bulrushes (*Scirpus validus*), Docks (*Rumexerispus* spp.), Dandelion (*Taraxacum officinale*) leaves, and Water Lily (*Nymphaea* spp.) pods.

There are many edible berries in the outdoors. It is a good idea to familiarize yourself with the identity of a specific few in order to eat them with complete safety. Also, these same edible berries provide the survivor with another commodity: teas. Blueberry (*Vaccinium* spp.), Raspberry, and Strawberry plants (*Fragaria* spp.), to name a few, certainly fall under this category. Their leaves, dried or fresh, when added to boiling water, produce a sweet tasting drink.

Many mushrooms are edible, delicious, and filling; however, bear in mind that some are extremely poisonous. As in the identification of edible plants, there are no rules which clearly differentiate "good" mushrooms from the poisonous variety. Unless you can positively identify a particular fungus, the risk of being poisoned far

Elderberry (Sambucus canadensis). Leaves from most edible berry plants, when boiled and steeped, produce tasty teas.

outweighs any nutrients gained. Although only five per cent of mushrooms could cause any serious harm, becoming sick in the wilds could conceivably tip the scales against the stranded victim.

Sap from trees is a good source of food. In the spring, trees such as the Maple (*Acer* spp.), Basswood (*Tilea americana*), and Birch (*Betula* spp.) provide a fast running sap which is like weak sugar water. Boiling this sap for a long period of time results in a nutritious, sticky syrup.

The cambium layer, or new growth layer, is found between the bark and the old wood. It can be scraped off and mashed into a pulp. This pulp is relatively tasty and contains some nutrients. Two good trees for this use are Hemlock (*Tsuga canadensis*) and Balsam Fir (*Abies balsamea*).

Lichens are dry, scaly-like plants usually found on exposed bed-rock or on old stumps. They can be eaten raw; however, they are best when first boiled and then dried. As thickeners for stew or soup, they are excellent. In a survival situation, it is to your advantage to make every effort to discover and utilize natural foods within your immediate area.

SOME OTHER PLANTS

Labrador Tea (*Ledum groenlandicum*) is a plant with a very wide distribution range. It is usually found in low-lying, damp, wooded areas. Boiling the leaves produces a very aromatic beverage similar to exotic teas. The best way to prepare this plant is

Fruit of Ground Cherry (Physalis spp.) is eaten raw or boiled.

to dry the leaves until they are easily crushed, then pouring hot water over the crushed leaves and allowing to steep. If in a hurry, simply rip the leaves apart and toss into boiling water. Labrador tea is high in vitamin C.

Lamb's-Quarters (*Chenopodium album*) is a field plant common throughout much of North America. Boil the young plant leaves just as you would spinach. Eaten raw, this plant makes an excellent salad.

Beach Pea (*Lathyrus japonicus*) is found on sandy, gravelly shores and beaches; it has a vetch-like look to it. Look for pinky-purple flowers, similar to pea blossoms. Raw or boiled, the peas are excellent.

The Pond Lily (*Nuphar* spp.), with its wide distribution, is a plant that is easily found. The roots may be eaten after being peeled and boiled. Seed pods can also be eaten and are best when newly formed. Boil them in two changes of water.

The Day Lily (*Hemerocallis fulva*) is a common field plant which has a recognizable large orange flower. Roots are eaten boiled or raw.

Silverweed (*Potentilla anserina*) is usually found in open fields. It has roots which are also good after boiling or roasting.

Lady's-Smock flowers (*Cardamine pratensis*) offer a tasty, pungent treat; however, since most specimens are unusual, beautiful, and fairly limited in distributuion, pick only when there are few options.

Dandelions and Cattails are two common plants easily recognized. Cattails grow in marshy or wet ground, often in swamps or drainage ditches beside the road. The flowering head can be eaten when young and green. Later, after turning brown, it may be crushed in order to produce Indian flour. The inner stem is a celery-like green and is widely used as a survival food. It is boiled or eaten raw. The root of Cattails is an excellent survival food as well. Bake, boil, or roast it. If the taste is too woody, masticate until it's like pulp, then swallow your starch-filled saliva, and spit out the residue. Dandelion, as was mentioned before, has leaves that are an excellent green. The roots can be dried and crushed to make a substitute for coffee.

Available all year round, Wintergreen (*Gaultheria procumbens*) leaves and berries can be eaten raw. Boiled, the leaves make a delicious, aromatic tea. This plant, a ground dweller and grows best in coniferous forests.

Leeks (*Allium tricoccum)* are found covering the moist floors of hardwood bush lots. They have a strong but tasty onion flavour. When cooking, use as the domestic onion, root, leaf, and all.
Knowing plants well is a fascinating and crucial part of wilderness survival. *It can also be quite dangerous, since some plants are extremely poisonous.*

We advise the novice to learn a few plants each year...*under the direction of a qualified instructor.*

MORE COMMON EDIBLE PLANTS: THE HOME VARIETY

All of us are familiar with the old adage that one (wo)man's food is another (wo)man's poison. Concerning useful and edible wild plants, this statement is of particular interest. Many of the plants mentioned here are as good as, if not better, than ordinary produce in terms of taste, nutrient value, and ease of preparation. The only problem is strictly mental; simply put, we are not in the habit of harvesting them; hence, instead of considering these plants as a food source, we view them as pests and weeds.

For the gardener, many of the weeds (s)he painstakingly pulls out and throws into the garbage bin can be better used as a supplement to the vegetables with which they compete. A classic example is Lamb's Quarters (also called Wild Spinach or Pokeweed). The "weed" is found in most gardens and is therefore despised. Unfortunately, many people do not realize that this plant tastes better and contains more nutrients than the domestic spinach!

Non-gardeners can gather and harvest many "weeds" along roadsides, fields, and some parks free for the taking. Generally speaking, these plants are fresher than the vegetables found in supermarkets; furthermore, they are free of the many chemicals used by growers to hasten growth or control insects.

WHAT IS A WEED?

Any plant not wanted or cultivated is generally referred to as a weed. We are all aware of the run-of-the-mill variety commonly found growing luxuriously in our lawns (mine included). One such example Is Plantain. Although we attempt to eradicate this pesky weed, it nonetheless seems to return every year. Many of us do not realize that Plantain's alter ego is Soldier's Herb. In the past, this plant was used as a poultice to disinfect cuts and wounds.

Another notorious weed is Chicory (*Cichorium intybus*). In no time, it seems to take over an entire lawn! A great deal of expense and effort are required to bring this pest under control. And yet, Chicory is a cultivated and relished plant in some European countries. During early spring, its leaves give salads a tangy taste; roots, when dried and crushed, have a flavour much akin to strong coffee.

Locally, we are blessed with a wide variety of other edible and useful plants. These include the Ox-eye Daisy (*Chrysanthemum leucanthemum*-eat the young leaves); Milkweed (fry the budding pods); Burdocks (*Arctium* spp. - prepare the roots like potatoes); Winter Cress (*Barbarea vulgaris* - use leaves in salads); Mints (teas); and Cattails (roots are prepared like potatoes, young shoots taste similar to celery, and tops can be made into flour).

I needn't tell anyone about the succulent taste of Fiddleheads (*Pteretis pensylvanica*) fried in butter, or the strong aroma of Wild Leeks. Many of us gather Raspberries or Blueberries (*Vaccinium* spp.), content with gorging ourselves on these luscious berries; however, we neglect to gather the leaves. Dried Raspberry and Blueberry leaves make an excellent tea.

CAUTION

Before gathering any plant, you are well advised to obtain permission from the landowner; furthermore, make certain that the area has not been sprayed with some toxic chemical. Harvesting the wild edible is a very rewarding pastime; it can also be quite lethal. Become well acquainted with the plant in question. If in doubt, do not gather. For example, Cowparsnip (*Heracleum maximum* - edible) is much akin to Water Hemlock (deadly poisonous). One is delicious; the other may kill you.

Finally, some plants leach heavy metals out of surrounding areas, and concentrate these particles in their root and leaf structures. Cattails are sometimes planted near industrial zones for this specific purpose. They extract iron, lead, and mercury from polluted ditches. In so doing, they clean up the local area.
If these plants are consumed, the results could prove fatal. Therefore, when harvesting, choose plants that grow in unpolluted streams and rivers.

NATIVE FOOD PLANTS: A SAMPLE

BUTTERNUT. (*Juglans cinerea*). The nuts were collected for two purposes. One was for the kernel which was eaten fresh or dried and stored for future use. The second use was for the dye obtained from the husks. The nuts are not quite as tasty as the Black Walnuts (*Juglans nigra*).

HAZELNUTS. (*Corylus* spp). The nuts of these shrubs were collected and used in much the same way that we use them today.

AMERICAN BEECH. (*Fagus grandifolia*). The kernels were used in a variety of ways. They were eaten fresh or stored for winter use. They were also dried and powdered to make flour for bread or cakes. The kernels also contain a good amount of oil and were crushed; the extracted oil was used for cooking purposes.

ACORNS. (*Quercus* spp). Acorns were an important source of flour for bread and other baking. The fresh nuts are bitter, but the Natives mixed the kernels with hardwood ashes and water and thus removed the bitter or astringent taste. Another technique was to powder the dried kernels and leach the flour with boiling water to remove the tannins. Some tribes buried acorns for a few days to remove that bitter taste.

RED MULBERRY. (*Morus rubra*). The large, red, juicy fruits were eaten fresh or dried and stored for winter use much as we do raisins.

WATER LILIES. (*Numphaea* spp). Anyone around shallow lake margins in the late summer will often see large, rounded rootstocks about as thick as a banana stem floating on the surface of the water. These are the roots of the Yellow Water Lily. They contain a considerable amount of starch and were an important source of food. They were boiled or roasted for immediate eating, or dried and powdered to make a flour. The large seeds of this lily were collected and roasted somewhat like popcorn although they did not burst open like popcorn. They were also dried and ground into flour.

WHITE WATER LILY. (*Nymphaea* spp). This Water Lily has large rootstocks which are rather tuber-like and about five or six cm long. These contain an abundance of starch and were used as a vegetable. The seeds were an important source of starchy materials for cooking. Look for them under water.

MAYAPPLE. (*Podophyllum peltatum*). The large, yellowish or greenish fruits are very good tasting at the proper stage of maturity. The pioneers also used them to make jam and preserves.

PEPPERWORT. (*Dentaria diphylla*). The thick, almost pencil-like rhizomes of this plant have a slight radish taste and are crisp and pleasant eating in the spring. The Natives collected them in quantity and allowed them to "ferment" for four or five days to dispel the acrid taste.

CURRANTS AND GOOSEBERRIES. (*Ribes* spp). These were eaten fresh or drled and stored for future use in cakes, bread or to mlx with pemmican.

RASPBERRIES, THIMBLEBERRIES, BLACKBERRIES, DEWBERRIES, all belong to the genus *Rubus*. All these delicious berries were eaten fresh or dried and stored for future use. Dried leaves were used to make teas.

STRAWBERRIES. (*Fraga*ria spp). Without doubt the Natives enjoyed strawberries as much as the white man; they were used in the same manner as other berry-like fruits.

WILD CHERRIES. (*Prunus* spp). These were collected in quantities and stored and beaten to a pulp. The poisonous hydrocyanic acid present in the pulverized stones was leached out. The pulp was then dried and used to flavour pemmican or other cooking.

CHOKEBERRIES. (*Pyrus* spp). The abundant reddish or black fruits have much the same flavour as the Choke-cherries. They contain considerable pectin and readily make a natural jelly; it was probably in this form that they were used by Natives.

JUNEBERRY, SHADBUSH, SERVICE BERRY. (*Amelanchier* spp.) The sweet, juicy fruits were collected and mashed to form a paste. This was dried and mixed with flour for bread or cakes, or mixed with pemmican for a special flavour.

GROUNDNUT. (*Apios americana*). This climbing plant has a chain of tuber-like enlargements two to four cm long, forming the root. In the fall, these are at their best and were dug up by the Natives and used in the same manner that we use potatoes; they were used fresh or stored for winter.

HOG PEANUT. (*Amphicarpa bracteata*). This plant produces underground flowers in the same manner as the peanut. These subterranean flowers, in autumn, develop somewhat bean-like, one-seeded fruits 1 to 2 cm in diameter. When properly cooked, they are said to taste like the garden bean.

SUGAR MAPLE. (*Acer saccharum*). Natives, like the white man, used the sap of the maple as a source of syrup, sugar, or just a sweet drink. Several maples produce sap which may be boiled down to syrup or sugar, but the common sugar or hard maple is the most popular.

Natives had various methods of preparing the sugar. They collected the sap in bark or wooden vessels and poured it into pots containing hot stones which evaporated the water. A second method was to allow the sap to freeze overnight. In the morning, the ice was removed and the thick, sugary syrup remained in the vessel.

The sapwood of the maple was used by a number of Native tribes as a source of bread flour. This bark was collected in the spring, dried, and pounded into a fine powder.

WILD GRAPE. (*Vitis* spp). Grapes are eaten fresh or dried and stored for winter use. Dried leaves are used to make teas.

CANADA BUFFALOBERRY. (*Shepherdia canadensis*). The red berries, when crushed, produce a red, soapy, foamy juice. This was sweetened and used much as we use jam or jelly.

WILD SPIKENARD. (*Aralia racemosa*). The thick roots were boiled or roasted for food. Apparently, they also had some medicinal value.

BLUEBERRIES, CRANBERRIES. (*Vaccinium* spp). The berries were eaten fresh or dried and stored for flavoring bread and cakes during the winter.

HUCKLEBERRIES. (*Gaylussacia* spp). These were used in the same manner as the Blueberries and Cranberries; also, they were often cooked and used as a delicacy or a sweetener. The stem was a source of fine fibres used in the making of thread, cord and fish lines.

ELDERBERRY. (*Sambucus canadensis*). The berries were used fresh or dried and stored.

ARROWHEADS. (*Sagittaria* spp). In the autumn, the plant produces hard, potato-like tubers two to four cm in diameter at the ends of the long underground runners. As fresh vegetables, they were roasted in hot ashes or boiled. For later use, they were boiled then sliced and strung on basswood strings.

WILD RICE. (*Zizania aquatica*). This was one of the best known and abundant foods of Natives. It inhabits shallow water, and, in the early fall, the Natives paddled into the rice areas, bent the tall stalks over their canoes, and beat out the grains. These were dried and stored for winter use; it was prepared much as we prepare rice.

BULRUSH. (*Scirpus validus*). These have stout, underground rootstocks containing considerable starch. The rootstocks were dried and pulverized and the resulting meal used as flour. The young roots, when boiled, produce a sweet syrup. The stems were used for weaving mats.

ARUM FAMILY. Most of the native members of the Arum family have thick, fleshy, underground rootsticks containing quantities of starch. In their fresh state, they are not edible because of the presence of crystals of calcium exalate which produce a violent stinging sensation in the mouth. However, when thoroughly dried, the acid taste disappears and the rootstocks were ground to a powder and used as flour. Some of the local members of the family that were used by the Natives are Jack-in-the-pulpit, (*Arisaema atrorubens*); Sweet Flag, (*Acorus calamus*); and Wild Calla, (*Calla palustris*).

WILD LEEK. (*Allium tricoccum*). The Native people sought the bulbs of this plant in the early spring. They were collected and dried for food and flavouring.

LICHENS. (*Cladonia* spp., *Parmelia* spp., and *Cetraria* spp.) Lichens were scraped off tree trunks, rocks, or branches and boiled. At times, they were cooked with meat to which they imparted a certain flavour. They were also reputed to be of medicinal value.

FIBRE PLANTS

SLIPPERY ELM. (*Ulmus rubra*). The inner bark was collected during the spring. It was cut into strips and shredded and made into rolls or coils. As needed, it was treated in the same manner as Basswood bark described below.

LEATHERWOOD. (*Dirca palustris*). Anyone who has tried to break a twig of Leatherwood will recognize its value as cordage. The bark is tough and flexible and was used by Natives for thongs.

BASSWOOD. (*Tilia americana*). The inner bark or bast of Basswood was probably one of the most common sources of fibre for the Natives. The bark of saplings was peeled off in the spring and the inner bark separated from the outer. It was then shredded to the desired size and rolled into balls or coiled. When string was required, these were boiled in lye water and the fibres separated. It was again rolled to break the fibrovascular bundles and finally twisted into string or rope or other necessities.

Basswood was also valuable for making the wooden vessels of the camp. It also produces the best type of wood to make firebow spindles. Finally, this wood was used for utensils; also the inner bark was used in basket-making.

DOGBANE AND INDIAN HEMP. (*Apocynum* spp). The outer bark of this semi-woody plant was peeled off. It was made into a very fine thread material. It was one of the sources of the Native bow strings.

MILKWEED. (*Asclepias syriaca*). The outer rind of Milkweed plants produce a very fine fibre. The bark or rind was stripped off, beaten, and woven; the resulting fibres were made into thread and string.

MISCELLANEOUS MATERIALS

CEDAR. (*Thuja occidentalis*). Sheets of cedar bark were used to cover lodges and longhouses. Dried, shredded bark was used as tinder.

TAMARACK, LARCH. (*Larix laricina*). The tough elastic roots of Tamarack were used by the Natives in making their birch bark canoes. After stripping off the bark, the root was steeped in water to make it more pliable. It was then coiled and put away ready for use.

SWEETFLAG. (*Acorus calamus*). The sweet, pleasant, vanilla-scented grass was widely used in the making of baskets and mats, braiding, and burned in some religious ceremonies.

BIRCH. *(Betula* spp.) The bark of the birches was used for many purposes but probably was best known for canoes; however, it was also used in the making of baskets, wigwam coverings, camp utensils, and as kindling. Sap, when fermented, produces Indian vinegar, ideal for sprinkling on salads and meats.

BEECH. *(Fagus grandifolia)*. Beech wood is a very durable, close-grained wood and was used extensively for camp utensils such as grinding bowls.

ASH. *(Fraxinus* spp.) The Natives were quite aware of the toughness of this wood and had many uses for it, especially basket-making.

Acorns from the Oak tree (Quercus spp.) are one of man's earliest food source.

SUMMARY: SOME EDIBLE AND USEFUL PLANTS

| | | SEASONS | | | | |
PLANTS	PART(S) USED	Spr.	Sum.	Fall	Winter	LOCATION
1. Alder (*Ulnus rugosa*)	a) buds	*				Poorly drained areas
	b) leaves	*	*			
2. Amaranths (*Amaranthus* spp.)	leaves	*	*	*		Field
3. Arrowheads (*Sagittaria* spp.)	roots	*	*	*		Water
4. Asparagus (*Asparagus officinalis*)	whole plant	*	*	*		Field
5. Balsam Fir (*Abies balsamea*)	a) gum	*	*	*	*	Forested
	b) cambium	*	*	*	*	
6. Bearberry (*Arctostaphylos uva-ursi*)	a) fruit		*	*		Dry Soils
	b) leaves	*	*	*		
7. Basswood (*Tilia americana*)	a) gum	*				Well drained soils
	b) flower	*				
8. Beech (*Fagus grandifolia*)	nuts		*	*		Well drained
9. Birches (*Betula* spp.)	a) leaves	*	*	*		Well drained
	b) buds	*				
	c) sap	*				
	d) cambium	*			*	

	PLANTS	PART(S) USED	Spr.	Sum.	Fall	Winter	LOCATION
10.	Blueberries (Vaccinium spp.)	a) fruit	*	*	*		Dry areas
		b) leaves	*	*			
11.	Bouncing Bet (Saponaria officinalis)	flower	*	*			Field
12.	Bugle Weed (Lycopus uniflorus)	roots		*	*		Wet areas
13.	Bulrush (Scirpus validus)	roots	*	*	*		Swamp
14.	Bunchberry (Cornus canadensis)	berries		*	*		Damp woodlands
15.	Burdocks (Arctium spp.)	a) roots	*	*	*		Field
		b) leaves (young)*					
16.	Butternut (Juglans cinerea)	nuts		*	*		Well drained
17.	Catnip (Nepeta cataria)	leaves	*	*	*		Field
18.	Cattails (Typha spp.)	a) pollen	*				Swamp
		b) stalk	*	*	*	*	
		c) roots	*	*	*		
19.	Cedar (Thuja ocidentalis)	a) needles	*	*	*	*	Wet areas
		b) cambium	*	*	*	*	
20.	Chamomile (Matricaria chamomilla)	a) flowers	*	*	*		Field
		b) leaves	*	*	*		

PLANTS	PART(S) USED	Spr.	Sum.	Fall	Winter	LOCATION
21. Cherry (*Prunus* spp.)	a) fruit		*	*		Well drained
	b) leaves	*	*			
22. Chestnut (*Castanea dentata*)	nut		*	*		Well drained
23. Chicory (*Cichorium intybus*)	a) roots	*	*	*		Field
	b) leaves	*	*	*		
24. Chickweeds (*Stellaria* spp.)	leaves	*	*	*		Open areas
25. Shrubby Cinquefoil (*Potentilla fruticosa*)	leaves	*	*	*		Field
26. Clovers (*Trifolium* spp.)	a) leaves	*	*	*		Field
	b) flowers	*	*	*		
27. Coltsfoot (*Tussilago farfara*)	leaves	*	*			Field
28. Corn-Lily (*Clintania borealis*)	leaves	*	*	*		Forested area
29. Cow-Parsnip (*Heracleum maximum*)	a) root	*	*	*		Well drained
	b) young leaves	*				
	c) flowering stalks	*	*			
30. Cowslip (*Caltha palustris*)	leaves	*				Streams, swamp

PLANTS	PART(S) USED	Spr.	Sum.	Fall	Winter	LOCATION
31. Crabapples (*Pyrus* spp.)	a) fruit	*	*	*		Well drained
	b) young leaves	*				
	c) bark	*			*	
32. Cranberry-High (*Viburnum trilobum*)	fruit		*	*		Wooded
33. Cranberry-Small (*Vaccinium oxycoccus*)	fruit			*		Wet areas, bogs
34. Curly Dock (*Rumex crispus*)	seed		*	*		Field
35. Currants (*Ribes* spp.)	a) fruit		*	*		Wet area
	b) leaves	*	*			
36. Daisy, Ox Eye (*Chrysanthemum leuchanthemum*)	a) leaves	*	*	*		Open area, fairly dry
	b) flower	*	*			
37. Dandelion (*Taraxacum officinale*)	a) flower	*	*			Field
	b) leaves	*	*	*		
	c) root	*	*	*		
38. Dog-Tooth Violet (*Erythronium americanum*)	leaves	*				Forested
39. Duddergrass (*Adiantum capillus-veneris*)	dried fronds		*	*		Moist woods

PLANTS	PART(S) USED	Spr.	Sum.	Fall	Winter	LOCATION
40. Elderberry (*Sambucus canadensis*)	fruit		*	*		Field
41. Elm, Slippery (*Ulmus rubra*)	a) inner bark	*	*	*	*	Field
	b) leaves	*	*	*		
42. False Solomon's Seal (*Smilacina racemosa*)	a) root	*	*	*		Wooded
	b) fruit		*	*		
	c) leaves	*	*			
43. Fern, Bracken (*Pteridium aguilinum*)	fiddlehead	*				Wooded
44. Fern, Ostrich (*Pteretis pensylvanica*)	fiddlehead	*				Wooded
45. Feverwort (*Triosteum perfoliatum*)	berries	*	*			Stony slopes
46. Fireweed (*Erechtites hieracifolia*)	a) leaves	*	*	*		Field
	b) pods		*	*		
	c) stalk	*	*			
47. Goldenrod, Sweet (*Solidago odora*)	flower		*	*		Field
48. Goldthread (*Coptis groenlandica*)	roots	*	*	*		Wooded
49. Gooseberries (*Ribes* spp.)	a) fruit		*	*		Field
	b) leaves	*	*	*		

PLANTS	PART(S) USED	Spr.	Sum.	Fall	Winter	LOCATION
50. Goosefoot (*Atriplex* spp.)	a) leaves b) fruit	*	* *			Field
51. Ground Cherries (*Physalis* spp.)	fruit		*			Field
52. Groundnut (*Apios americana*)	a) seeds b) tuber	*	* *	* *		Damp soils
53. Hawthorns (*Crataegus* spp.)	a) fruit b) leaves	*	* *	* *	*	Field
54. Hazelnuts (*Corylus* spp.)	nut		*	*		Wooded
55. Hemlock (*Tsuga canadensis*)	a) leaves b) cambium	* *	* *	* *	* *	Wooded
56. Hickories (*Carya* spp.)	nuts		*	*		Wooded
57. Horsetail (*Equisetum* spp.)	whole plant - shoots	*	*	*		Field
58. Jack-In-The-Pulpit (*Arisaema atrorubens*)	roots	*	*	*		Wooded
59. Jerusalem Artichoke (*Helianthus tuberosus*)	roots		*	*		Field

167

PLANTS	PART(S) USED	Spr.	Sum.	Fall	Winter	LOCATION
60. Juniper, Ground (*Juniperus communis*)	a) leaves	*	*	*	*	Field
	b) berries	*	*	*	*	
61. Labrador Tea (*Ledum groenlandicum*)	leaves	*	*	*	*	Wet areas
62. Lamb's-Quarters (*Chenopodium album*)	a) leaves	*	*	*		Field
	b) seeds		*	*		
63. Leeks (*Allium* spp.)	a) roots	*	*	*		Wooded
	b) leaves	*	*			
64. Lichens (*Cladonia, Parmelia,* & *Cetraria* spp.)	whole plant	*	*	*	*	*Woods, Fields*
65. Licorice Root (*Hedysarum* spp.)	root	*	*	*		Poorly drained areas
66. Maple (*Acer* spp.)	a) leaves	*	*	*	*	Well drained, damp areas
	b) cambium	*	*	*		
	c) sap	*				
	d) buds	*				
67. Mayapple (*Podophyllum peltatum*)	fruit		*			Wooded
68. Milkweed (*Asclepias syriaca*)	a) pods			*		Field
	b) flowers	*	*			

168

PLANTS	PART(S) USED	SEASONS				LOCATION
		Spr.	Sum.	Fall	Winter	
69. Mint, Wild (*Mentha arvensis*)	leaves	*	*	*		Wet areas
70. Mosses (*Umbilicaria* spp.)	whole plant	*	*	*	*	Trees, rocks damp areas
71. Mountain Ash (*Pyrus* spp.)	fruit		*	*		Field
72. Mulberry, Red (*Morus rubra*)	a) fruit	*	*			Field
	b) leaves		*	*		
73. Mullein, Common (*Verbascum thapsus*)	leaves	*	*	*	*	Field
74. Mustards, Wild (*Brassica* spp.)	a) leaves	*	*	*		Field
	b) seeds		*	*		
75. Nutgrass (*Cyperus esculentus*)	tubers	*	*	*		Rich, moist soils
76. Oaks (*Quercus* spp.)	acorn		*	*	*	Well drained
77. Onion, Wild (*Allium stellatum*)	a) roots	*	*	*		Wooded
	b) leaves	*	*			
78. Orache (*Atriplex patula*)	a) leaves	*	*			Wet flats
	b) seeds			*		
79. Pickerelweed (*Pontederia cordata*)	fruit		*	*		Water

PLANTS	PART(S) USED	Spr.	Sum.	Fall	Winter	LOCATION
80. Pines (*Pinus* spp.)	a) cambium	*	*	*	*	Dry soils
	b) seeds		*	*	*	
81. Plantains (*Plantago* spp.)	a) leaves	*	*			Field
	b) seeds		*	*		
82. Pokeweed (*Phytolacca americanna*)	young leaves	*	*			Field
83. Poplars (*Populus* spp.)	a) bark	*	*	*	*	Field, wooded
	b) leaves	*	*	*		
84. Prickly Lettuce (*Lactuca scariola*)	leaves	*	*			Field
85. Primrose, Evening (*Oenothera biennis*)	a) roots	*	*	*		Field
	b) leaves	*	*			
86. Purslane (*Portulaca oleracea*)	a) seeds	*	*	*		Sandy soils
	b) whole plant	*	*	*		
87. Queen Anne's Lace (*Daucus carota*)	a) roots	*	*	*		Field
	b) leaves	*	*	*		
88. Raspberries (*Rubus* spp.)	a) fruit		*			Field
	b) leaves	*		*		
89. Rock Tripe (*Umbilicaria* spp.)	whole plant	*	*	*	*	Rocks

	PLANTS	PART(S) USED	Spr.	Sum.	Fall	Winter	LOCATION
				SEASONS			
90.	Sarsaparilla (Aralia racemosa)	roots	*	*	*		Wooded, damp
91.	Saxifrage, Lettuce (Saxifraga micranthidifolia)	leaves	*	*			Moist meadows
92.	Serviceberries (Amelanchier spp.)	fruit	*	*			Well drained
93.	Sheep Sorrel (Rumex acetosella)	leaves	*	*			Field
94.	Shepherd's Purse (Capsellara bursapastoris)	a) leaves	*	*	*		Open areas
		b) seeds	*	*			
95.	Silverweed (Potentilla anserina)	a) roots	*	*	*		Damp soils
		b) leaves	*	*	*		
96.	Solomon's Seal (Polygonatum spp.)	a) roots	*	*	*		Wooded
		b) shoots	*				
97.	Spring Beauties (Claytonia spp.)	roots	*	*	*		Wooded
98.	Spruces (Picea spp.)	a) gum	*	*	*	*	Forested, moist
		b) leaves	*	*	*	*	
		c) cambium	*		*	*	
99.	Stinging Nettle (Urtica dioica)	leaves	*	*	*		Well drained

PLANTS	PART(S) USED	Spr.	Sum.	Fall	Winter	LOCATION
100. St. John's Wort (*Hypericum perforatum*)	leaves	*	*	*		Field
101. Strawberries, Wild (*Fragaria* spp.)	a) leaves	*	*	*		Well drained
	b) fruit	*	*			
102. Sumac, Staghorn (*Rhus typhina*)	fruit			*	*	Well drained
103. Sweet Flag (*Acorus calamus*)	stalk	*	*	*	*	Damp soils
104. Tamarack (*Larix laricina*)	a) needles	*	*	*	*	Poorly drained soils
	b) cambium	*	*	*		
105. Tansy, Common (*Tanacetum vulgare*)	leaves	*	*	*		Field
106. Thistle, Bull (*Cirsium vulgare*)	leaves	*	*	*		Field
107. Thistle, Sow (*Sonchus oleraceus*)	shoots	*				Field
108. Tinker's-Weed (*Triosteum perfoliatum*)	berries		*	*		Wooded
109. Toothworts (*Dentaria* spp.)	roots	*	*	*		Wet and well drained areas
110. Touch-Me-Not (*Impatiens pallida*)	a) flower	*	*	*		Damp
	b) leaves	*	*			

PLANTS	PART(S) USED	Spr.	Sum.	Fall	Winter	LOCATIONS
111. Twisted Stalk (*Streptopus amplexifolius*)	berry		*	*		Wooded
112. Veronica (*Veronica* spp.)	leaves	*	*	*		Moist areas
113. Violet, Blue (*Viola papilionacea*)	a) flower	*	*			Woods
	b) leaves	*	*			
114. Yarrow (*Achillea millefolium*)	a) flower	*	*	*		Field
	b) leaves		*	*		
115. Yellow Goat's Beard (*Tragopogon Pratensis*)	a) roots	*	*	*		Field
	b) shoots	*				
116. Watercress (*Nasturtium officinale*)	whole plant	*	*	*	*	Water
117. Water Lilies (*Nymphaea* spp.)	roots	*	*	*		Water
118. Wild Calla (*Calla palustris*)	fruit	*	*	*		Water
119. Wild Garlic (*Allium canadense*)	whole plant	*	*	*		Wooded
120. Wild Ginger (*Asarum canadense*)	roots	*	*	*		Wooded
121. Wild Grapes (*Vitis* spp.)	a) leaves	*	*	*		Wooded, well drained
	b) fruit		*	*	*	

PLANTS	PART(S) USED	Spr.	Sum.	Fall	Winter	LOCATION
122. Wild Plums (*Prunus* spp.)	a) fruit	*	*	*	*	Field
	b) leaves		*	*		
123. Wild Rice (*Zizania aquatica*)	grain		*	*		Water
124. Wild Rose (*Rosa* spp.)	a) buds	*				Field
	b) hips		*	*	*	
	c) leaves	*	*	*		
125. Willows (*Salix* spp.)	a) leaves	*	*	*		Poorly drained areas
	b) bark	*	*	*	*	
126. Winter Cress (*Barbarea vulgaris*)	a) seeds	*	*	*		Field
	b) leaves		*	*		
127. Winter Green (*Gaultheria procumbens*)	a) leaves	*	*	*		Forested
	b) berries	*	*	*	*	
128. Wood-Sorrel, Common (*Oxalis montana*)	leaves	*	*			Forested

SUGGESTED READING

Angier, B. *Feasting Free On Wild Edibles*. New York: Pyramid Books, 1977.

Burt, C., and Heyl, F.G. *Edible and Poisonous Plants Of The Eastern States*. Portland: Science Sales.

Burt, C., and Heyl, F.G. *Edible and Poisonous Plants Of The Western States*. Portland: Science Sales.

Chase, M.C. *Field guide to Edible and Useful Plants of North America*. Redwing: Nature Study Aids Inc..

Coon, N. *The Dictionary of Useful Plants*. Emmaus: Rodale Press, 1974.

Coon, N. *Using Wayside Plants*. New York: Hearthside Press, 1969.

Dermek, A. *Mushrooms and Other Fungi*. Chichester: Autumn Publishing, 1982.

Edible And Poisonous Mushrooms. Ottawa: Information Canada, 1976.

Ferri, G. *Eating Out*. Thunder Bay: Lakehead U. Press, 1984.

Gibbons, E. *Stalking The Wild Asparagus*. New York: David McKay Co., 1962.

Hardin, J.W. and Arena, J.M. *Human Poisoning From Native & Cultivated Plants*. North Carolina: Duke Univ. Press, 1969.

Harris, B.C. *Eat the Weeds*. Barre: Barre Publishing, 1968.

Kingsbury, J.M. *Poisonous Plants of United States and Canada*. Englewood Cliffs: Prentice Hall, 1964.

Kunzle, J. *Herbs and Weeds*. Switzerland: Minusio - Locarno, 1971.

Medsger, O.P. *Edible Wild Plants*. New York: MacMillan, 1972.

Mohney, R. *Why Wild Edibles?* Seattle: Pacific Search, 1975.

Mushroom Collecting For Beginners. 20M-36866-7:74, Ottawa: Information Canada, 1974.

Native Trees of Canada. F045-61-1969-1, Ottawa: Information Canada, 1975.

Ontario Weeds. Guelph: Ontario Agricultural College, 1977.

Peterson, L. *Field Guide to Edible Wild Plants*. Boston: Houghton, 1978.

Smith, A.H. *The Mushroom Hunter's Field Guide*. The University of Michigan Press.

Sweet, M. *Common Edible and Useful Plants of the West*. Heraldsburg.

Turner, N.J. *Food Plants of British Columbia Indians Part I Coastal Peoples*. British Columbia Provincial Museum Handbook #34, 1975.

Weiner, M.A. *Earth Medicines, Earth Foods*. New York: Macmillan, 1972.

DOGTOOTH VIOLET, *(Erythronium americanum)*

CHAPTER 6

It is one of the most beautiful compensations of this life that no man can sincerely try to help another without first helping himself.

- Shakespeare

PSYCHOLOGY OF THE INJURED PERSON

STAGES

When an accident occurs, it is often a traumatic shock for everyone concerned. For the victim(s), there is normally a general reaction pattern. Depending on the individual(s), any of the five stages may last longer than others. Immediately following a mishap:

There is usually a period of <u>alarm</u>. This is an emotional reaction. The victim realizes that the unexpected has happened.

This is followed by a period of <u>threat</u>, a time when critical decisions must be made. What is to be done?

A period of <u>impact</u> finally hits the victim. He comes to the realization that a problem exists. Some members of the party take charge.

Later, a period of <u>inventory</u> takes hold. The victim assesses the situation. Again, strong and different emotional responses surface.

Finally, there is a period of <u>rescue</u>. At this stage, first aid is administered.

REACTION TYPES

A victim's reaction to a traumatic experience is normally unpredictive; however, there are six basic responses at the scene of an accident:

Normal	- accident victims are afraid and excited.
Panic	- individuals completely lose all sense of good judgement.
Overactivity	- characterized by people aimlessly moving around.
Grief	- mental anguish; victims are too sad to do anything.

177

| Depression | - these victims are unresponsive to all stimuli. |

| Physical disorders | -psychological deafness or blindness may paralyze some members of the party. |

In any case, the injured party will be in shock and experiencing fear.

RESPONSE OF THE FIRST AIDER

It is imperative that the first aider cope with his own reactions. If he's a group leader, he must not only handle the reactions of his members, he must also control the activities of the injured. In essence, the rescuer must:
   a) Relax. Be assuring and calm; check for priorities, constantly talk to the patients; and take full control of the situation.

   b) Evaluate the situation: do so systematically, quietly, and carefully; check for any immediate dangers; take full control. If necessary, use the most trusted and able members in the group.

   c) Always keep personal emotions under control. Remain calm, no matter what the circumstances; be aloof, yet in full control; don't be too close to the action, otherwise, the first aider may lose the overall perspective of the situation.

   d) Be honest, but not blunt. Do not lie to the victim.

   e) Avoid the use of force. Be calm, use gentle, but firm, persuasion.

HANDLING TYPES OF REACTIONS

The first aider must gently and firmly handle the victims of an accident. Tragedies which take place in an urban centre are bad enough; however, in a wilderness setting, the problem is compounded: there is no immediate ambulance response. Help may be hours away; the victim is surrounded by unfamiliar sounds and surroundings; the weather, environment, and geographic features may further compound the situation; and members of the accident party may be overly fatigued and exhausted.

Each type of reaction must be handled in different fashion:

Normal - offer encouragement to the victim.

Panic - treat with gentle firmness; ask others for help.

Depression - give assurance; make these casualties feel that they're a part of the group.

Overactivity - put them to work doing any worthwhile activity.

Grief - if a death has occurred, separate bereaved from the deceased and share his feelings;

Physical disorders - suggest a series of small tasks for them to perform.

COLD WEATHER INJURIES

DEEP FROSTBITE

Frostbite is simply the freezing of some part of the body. It is likely to occur in sub-freezing weather particularly when there is a cold wind.

SIGNS AND SYMPTOMS

Frostbite can usually be seen before it is felt. People exposed to subfreezing weather should help each other by watching for the tell-tale spots on the other person. The skin becomes dull and whitish; there is a numbness or prickling associated with the formation of ice crystals in the tissues but no pain is felt by the victim. Later, tissues become solid and immovable upon freezing. Eventually, any prolonged exposure to cold causes a person to become numb and drowsy; his eyesight fails; he becomes unconscious and his respiration may cease. He is already a casualty and unable to help himself.

It is easier to prevent frostbite or stop it in its very early stages than to thaw and take care of badly frozen flesh.

PREVENTION

Always dress appropriately for the weather, and have extra clothing should the weather change. If at all possible, always keep dry. In extremely low temperatures, be careful not to touch metal with bare skin, since flesh will freeze to the metal. On the trail, continually exercise exposed parts of your body. Wiggle your face, fingers, and toes from time to time in order to keep them warm. Move your ears with your hand in order to increase circulation to that area. Finally, use the buddy system. Watch your partner's face to see if any whitish spots show; and have him watch yours. Thaw frozen spots immediately using bare hands or other sources of body heat.

TREATMENT

If there is any danger of re-freezing, do not attempt to thaw the frozen skin. Instead, wait until this problem has been solved. As quickly as possible, get the victim into some type of heated shelter, but do not warm the frozen part too rapidly, and do not use local or direct heat. Avoid interference with the circulation by constriction; therefore, be careful when wrapping frozen extremities in blankets or clothing for transportation. If in an heated shelter, leave limbs exposed at room temperature, preferably not higher than 25 degrees Celsius. Avoid the pressure of blankets on frost-bitten extremities. Do not open blisters. If victim is conscious, encourage warm drinks and food. Only in cases of prolonged exposure to severe cold should rapid warming of the body be undertaken. Use artificial respiration if necessary.

The utilization of body heat is one of the most effective ways to aid thawing. The use of armpits and groin should be considered since they are generally warm, comfortable cavities. If the frostbite is accompanied by breaks in the skin, apply sterile dressings. Never use strong antiseptics such as tincture of iodine or powdered sulfa drugs on the wound.

Rubbing frostbite may tear frozen tissues and cause further damage. Do not apply snow or ice since this merely accentuates the injury. Do not soak frozen limbs in kerosene or oil for the same reason.

Exercising frozen parts will increase tissue damage and is likely to break the skin, therefore protect and immobilize the damaged areas. Using a litter or sled to evacuate in cases of frozen lower extremities will help prevent further injuries. Use a casualty evacuation bag if one is available.

HYPOTHERMIA

Consider this scenario:

A hiker is preparing for a leisurely walk through a familiar forest. A casual glance out the window shows a sunny and warm day. The hiker, unsuspecting any weather change, dresses accordingly, neglecting to take along any food, extra clothing, or rain gear. Enthusiastically, he sets out.

Part way through the hike the weather takes a turn: the winds pick up, the blue sky is slowly replaced by dark menacing clouds, and the temperature drops considerably. The hiker is feeling sensations of hunger but is reluctant to stop, for the pace is going well and the pre-determined distance must be covered! Almost unnoticeably, the newly arrived clouds release a gentle drizzle. Undoubtingly, the hiker believes this to be temporary, and nothing to worry over.

Slowly this drizzle turns into light rain. The wind begins to pick up. This is a deadly combination for someone who is tired, hungry and unprepared. A keen observer would notice the first signs of hypothermia ... a cold sensation, skin numbness, minor impairment in use of the hands, and some uncontrolled shivering.

The hiker dismisses these signs as normal hardships to be endured and nothing more. He moves on. Time passes, and the day darkens; the weather is unyielding. The hiker's pace slows down. He now displays signs of muscle unco-ordination, along with mild confusion. He's still unaware that he's suffering from hypothermia. Soon, he begins to stumble frequently, falling constantly and is unable to effectively use his hands; he's slow in thought, and slurs his speech. And yet, the hiker, in an obvious state of anxiety, still makes no effort to stop and rest. He is not aware that this is the final stage where he can help himself. If his condition worsens, the victim will be in no position to recover without outside aid.

Eventually, the victim's condition steadily deteriorates; he's incoherent, confused, and irrational; severe shivering is apparent, along with muscle unco-ordination; he can no longer stand or walk.

Self-help is no longer possible! Outside aid must be obtained if he's going to survive. Soon, muscle rigidity, dilation of the pupils, and semi-consciousness sets in. His heart beat and pulse diminishes in strength. Unconsciousness and death are inevitable.

This scenario illustrates how subtly hypothermia can develp and overcome any outdoorsperson.

And what is hypothermia? It is the lowering of the body's core temperature to a level at which the functioning capacity of muscular and cerebral systems are impaired; it is excessive heat loss, exceeding heat production resulting from an overwhelming exposure to the outdoor elements. If left untreated, death will result. Basically, there are two categories of hypothermia: acute and chronic. Acute refers to the sudden drop in body temperature. This is caused by the rapid immersion of the body in very cold waters. Chronic is the more common type often experienced by outdoorspeople. In this case, its approach is very slow. It is usually caused by radiation (exposed parts of the body, such as head and arms), conduction (sitting on cold ground), or by convection (exposure to cold winds).

To understand the concept of thermoregulation, envisage the body as a cylinder having an inner core and an outer insulating shell. The inner core consists of the vital organs, that is, the brain, heart, lungs, liver, and kidneys; its temperature is a constant 37 degrees C.

The outer shell is composed of skin, fat, muscle, ligaments, tendons, and appendages; its temperature can drop to as low as 33 degrees C.

Our metabolism ensures the steady conversion of foods to energy and heat. In other words, think of the body as a furnace. The fuel (food) is processed into heat. Without food, therefore, the body cannot continue producing heat and energy.

When cold, we shiver. This is the body's attempt to increase heat production. By shivering, we generate six times as much heat; if we exercise, the body produces 20 times the amount of heat output.

In the event that the inner core area cannot maintain its 37 degrees C. temperature, it attempts to reduce heat loss. It therefore withdraws heat (circulation) from the outer shell, thus conserving heat for the central core. The body is willing to sacrifice parts of its outer shell (ears, fingers, toes) in a desperate effort to protect the internal organs.

As seen in this scenario, a victim can be over-whelmed by the cold, wind, and wetness. The body cannot effectively thermoregulate itself without proper protection, food and rest. The result is hypothermia.

Incidentally, hypothermia can easily affect individuals without the physical capacities to adequately maintain a constant core temperature of 37 degrees C. This includes the very young and the very old. Impaired (alcohol, drugs, or sickness) people are also very susceptible to hypothermia.

When venturing in the outdoors, we strongly advise individuals to be prepared for any weather change specific to their region. Outdoor persons are encouraged to carry extra clothing such as loose-fitting woolen shirts, sweaters and pants. A proper raincoat is mandatory. They should have extra food, drinks, and snacks for that added energy in case it's needed. Everyone should be familiar with the signs of hypothermia. When travelling with others, be alert for early symptoms. Ask yourself: Is that person weak, forgetful, slightly confused because he's tired? Or is he demonstrating the early signs of hypothermia? Even if the individual is hypothermic, he may deny the fact and refuse all help. The first aider must be diplomatic, yet forceful.

When symptoms do appear, immediately shelter the victim from wind and rain. Use whatever is available, eg. tent, tarp, rain gear or natural shelter. The victim is losing more heat than he can produce. All wet clothing must be removed immediately. The victim should have all exposed skin covered. Take special care to keep him off the cold ground. Assistance will be needed in replacing lost body heat. To do so effectively, have one person place his bare chest to the victim's bared chest; another places his chest to the victim's back. Keep everyone covered with blankets or sleeping bags. If available, apply hot water-filled plastic containers to the victim's underarms and groin. If conscious, offer the victim warm liquids.

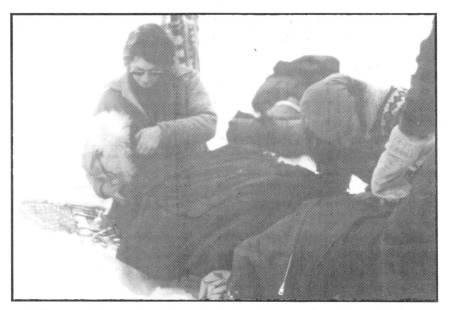

When treating an hypothermic victim, place any additional or extra clothing under the casualty to insulate him from the cold ground.

Move the victim very slowly, since sudden, rapid moves may induce cardiac arrest. Once recovered, keep the patient under close surveillance. Continue to offer warm liquids and verbal support.

During the Korean war, some apparently lifeless soldiers were left lying on the frozen battlefields. Since medics were unable to detect a pulse on the wrists and legs, these soldiers were thought to be dead. Later, it was discovered that these victims were hypothermia cases. The body had stopped all blood circulation to the extremeties; hence, no pulse! When hypothermia is concerned, the first aider should always take a pulse at the throat area.

BODY TEMPERATURE: PATHOPHYSIOLOGY

Normal   37 - 35 degrees Celsius
                   Alert;
                   Intense and uncontrollable shivering;
                   Some impairment in muscular performance especially in use of hands.

               35 - 33 degrees Celsius
                   Violent shivering;
                   Speech difficulty;
                   Confusion, sluggish thinking, beginning of amnesia;

183

Slow stumbling pace.
Delirium, apathy, and depression.

33 - 30 degrees Celsius
Shivering decreases then stops;
Muscular rigidity, erratic jerky movements;
Irrationality;
Total amnesia possible;
Skin blue or puffy;
Victim usually retains posture and some contact with the environment

30 - 27 degrees Celsius
Stupor, irrationality, muscular rigidity, pulse and respiration slowed;
Pupils dilated;
Coma, Cardiac arrhythmia

27 - 26 degrees Celsius
Unconsciousness;
Most reflexes cease to function;
Erratic heart beat. Appears lifeless

Below 26 degrees Celsius
Failure of cardiac, respiratory control centres in brain;
Cardiac fibrillation or arrest;
Edema and hemorrhage in lungs - death
Artificial respiration is not recommended.

WIND SPEED

Calm	Trees are motionless, smoke rises vertically
Below 20 k	Small branches on trees move, can feel wind.
Up to 35 k	Larger branches move, snow swirls over drifts
Above 40 kph	Largest branches move, tree trunks move, wind whistles and walking into wind is difficult.

MAMMALIAN DIVING REFLEX

Acute hypothermia in cold water may be combined with "near drowning". Although the term drowning refers to expiration, near drowning describes an individual who has been underwater, unconscious, and is not breathing.

A great deal of research has been done in this general area. Dr. Martin Nemiroff, University of Michigan Hospital, has repeatedly shown that after four minutes without oxygen, irreversible and permanent brain damage does not necessarily take place. He has documented the survival rate of many victims who were submerged under cold water (below 20°), from four to thirty-eight minutes. These individuals recovered without suffering brain damage.

This is due to a phenomenom called mammalian diving reflex. Simply put, this takes place when a mammal is submerged into cold water. The body reduces the oxygen needs in all tissues, and decreases all blood flow to the skin, muscles, and other organs. This act reserves the precious supply of oxygen, carried via warm blood, for the brain.

How does this data effect our rescue efforts? The message is quite clear - do not give up on direct artificial respiration and C.P.R.; don't stop after four or five minutes - keep going, for as long as it takes.

All hypothermics should be re-warmed. There was a case in the Massachusetts General Hospital (Boston) whereby a patient haveing a core temperature of only 17°C was successfully revived. So don't give up!

Other research has accentuated a proper method of removing victims from cold water. If someone has been immersed for sometime, (s)he should be lifted out in an horizontal position; this decreases the possibility of a sudden vascual collapse.

WIND MPH (miles per hour)	TEMPERATURE (degrees Fahrenheit)																				
	40	35	30	25	20	15	10	5	0	-5	-10	-15	-20	-25	-30	-35	-40	-45	-50	-55	-60
	EQUIVALENT CHILL TEMPERATURE																				
5	35	30	25	20	15	10	5	0	-5	-10	-15	-20	-25	-30	-35	-40	-45	-50	-55	-60	-70
10	30	20	15	10	5	0	-10	-15	-20	-25	-35	-40	-45	-50	-60	-65	-70	-75	-80	-90	-95
15	25	15	10	0	-5	-10	-20	-25	-30	-40	-45	-50	-60	-65	-70	-80	-85	-90	-100	-105	-110
20	20	10	5	0	-10	-15	-25	-30	-35	-45	-50	-60	-65	-75	-80	-85	-95	-100	-110	-115	-120
25	15	10	0	-5	-15	-20	-30	-35	-45	-50	-60	-65	-75	-80	-90	-95	-105	-110	-120	-125	-135
30	10	5	0	-10	-20	-25	-30	-40	-50	-55	-65	-70	-80	-85	-95	-100	-110	-115	-125	-130	-140
35	10	5	-5	-10	-20	-30	-35	-40	-50	-60	-65	-75	-80	-90	-100	-105	-115	-120	-130	-135	-145
40	10	0	-5	-15	-20	-30	-35	-45	-55	-60	-70	-75	-85	-95	-100	-110	-115	-125	-130	-140	-150

Winds above 40 mph have little additional effect	LITTLE DANGER	INCREASING DANGER (flesh may freeze within one minute)	GREAT DANGER (flesh may freeze within 30 seconds)

SNOWBLINDNESS

Snow can reflect back to the eye as much as 85 to 90 percent of all light falling on it. Very short periods of exposure to this intense glare can result in snowblindness, a disabling and very painful experience.

EMERGENCY GOGGLES: BARK AND WOODEN SAMPLES

Birch bark goggles are simple to make and offer emergency eye protection from the sun's rays.

Birch bark goggles should be cut from a thick piece of bark, approximately 20 cm long and 4 cm wide. The slits are placed directly in front of the eyes; they're very thin but fairly long.

Use any string or shoelace to fasten around the head.

Wooden goggles, although more difficult to make, offer better protection.

Cut from any soft woods, including cedar, poplar, or pine.

Birch bark goggles are relatively easy to fashion.

Wooden goggles, although more difficult to make, offer better protection.

Snowblindness is the result of ultraviolet rays burning the conjunctiva of the eye. (The conjunctiva is the delicate membrane which lines the eyelids and covers the exposed surface of the eyeball.) You can become "snowblinded" on sunny days, on overcast days and even on days of light fog. During overcast days, light is reflected back and forth between cloud ceiling and snow. The absence of shadows causes the ground to look level. This leads to eyestrain, which makes the eyes more susceptible to snowblindness.

The only effective prevention of snowblindness is sunglasses, preferably goggles of the side-blinder type which prevent reflected light from coming in at the bottom and sides. Glasses should be worn out-of-doors at all times when the sun is above the horizon. Be sure the metal parts of metal frame sunglasses do not touch your face and lead to frostbite. If they do touch your face, wrap them with something such as bandaids or electrician's tape.

There is no such thing as a warning symptom of snowblindness to alert you; it only takes 2 to 12 hours to develop. By the time you experience the symptoms, it is too late. Symptoms are:
- Severe pain due to swelling of the conjunctiva
- Extreme sensitivity to light
- Watering of the eyes
- Smarting eyelids
- Headache and depression

The ideal treatment for snowblindness is rest in a darkened area with bandaged eyes and cold compresses for pain for 1 to 5 days. Treatment consists of staying in a dark shelter or wearing a lightproof bandage. If the situation dictates, the snowblinded survivor can be blind-folded and led.

To relieve the pain of snowblindness, take aspirin (or Tylenol) and use cold compresses on the eyes if there is no danger of freezing. Do not use eyedrops or ointment. Most cases of snowblindness will recover within 18 hours without medical treatment but the first attack of snowblindness is said to make the victim more susceptible to other attacks.

If you should lose or break your sunglasses, you can improvise Inuit goggles by cutting or burning slits in wood, bark, cardboard or similar material. Inuit goggles have the advantage of not frosting over but they do limit your field of vision.

Blacking your nose and the area around your eyes and looking at dark objects as you travel help somewhat to reduce the effects of glare in a snow environment, but these measures do not prevent snowblindness.

DRESSING FOR THE OUTDOORS: LAYERING

The origins of the layering can be traced back to poverty stricken classes which inhabited colder areas. Simply put, the poor did not have the luxury of owning special clothing for winter months; thus, when harsh weather arrived, they utilized all of their garments to keep warm. The rudiments of what we know today as the layering principle was, in all probability, pioneered by these people. How does this principle work?

Dead air pockets are formed between layers of loosely fitting clothes; hence, more layers create more air pockets. With a properly insulated body, the core's warmth is maintained in all the extremities. Layering allows one to remove as many items of clothing as is required to release excess heat, a procedure that minimizes wetness of the body. A damp body in cold weather leads to rapid cooling; it saturates clothing, thereby diminishing any of the clothing's original insulative value.

On the other hand, layering allows one to replace the number of garments needed to keep warm.
This system is superior to wearing the more popular, bulky, one-piece garment such as snowmobile suit. When removing a cumbersome one-piece garment, the individual is left with nothing more than a shirt or sweater.

The style and type of clothing with which one layers is as important as the layering system itself. Exorbitant amounts of heat escape from the chest area; body heat escapes through zippers and other gaps in garments that utilize buttons; therefore, it would seem advantageous to layer with closed garments. This includes sweaters or long anaraks. This type of clothing will lock warm air between its layers. In accordance with the Inuit style, the length of this outer garment should extend below one's waist. This added length will keep the cold-sensitive kidneys warm, and when walking, the garment tends to flop around, thereby providing ventilation; this minimizes moisture build-up.

Many experienced outdoors people believe that wool's properties elevate it above most materials. Wool enhances the layering principle! Its structure, being lofty, enables wool to trap endless pockets of air. Also, it contains natural oils which further add to its insulative qualities. One other useful property of wool is its ability to retain loft even when wet. Finally, wool is relatively cheap, durable and readily accessible to most outdoor enthusiasts.

In the case of those who wear T-shirts next to their skin, a further problem is created: T-shirts retain body moisture for a lengthy period of time! This keeps the person perpetually cold!

In the outdoors, the greatest robber of body heat is convection. Wind whistles about one's body, swiftly stealing precious body heat and replacing it with cold air. A good wind breaker is advisable. As previously mentioned, it is more advantageous to wear a close-faced windbreaker rather than the more popular zipper type.

Many inexperienced outdoors people are thought to be well dressed for the conditions, yet they're still cold simply because of the absence of good head wear. Wearing a wool hat is advisable. This often makes the difference between being comfortably warm or dreadfully cold. By reducing heat loss, hats aid in extending body core warmth to the extremities.

Other points to consider in relation to proper bush dress includes wearing suspenders instead of belts. Belts constrict circulation of air and blood; suspenders allow air to circulate, thus, drying the body through ventilation.

Avoid wearing gloves, since they separate the fingers, causing them to become cold. Instead, wear mittens. In this way, fingers will be in contact with each other, thereby keeping themselves warm.

Apply the layering principle to the feet. Wear two or three layers of thinner, woolen socks instead of one large, bulky pair. Socks should be changed regularly due to the lack of proper foot ventilation. One's winter boots should be reasonably loose fitting; that is, toes must have the freedom of movement. Avoid steel-toed boots; they conduct warmth away from the feet.

Finally, the reader is advised to experiment with these suggestions. In so doing, (s)he will tailor our comments to suit his/her individual needs.

PERSONAL WELFARE: THE SEARCH PARTY

The immediate treatment of a victim could be the deciding factor in his survival. In other words, members of the search party should have the knowledge to treat the lost individual wherever he may be located. The rescuer must have an excellent repertoire of wilderness first aid skills. Hence, he will be able to recognize the signs and symptoms immediately and begin treatment in the field.

We caution the search party, however, to expect anything when on a mission. Members must be prepared for bad weather and should:
>-wear adequate clothing, dress in layers, regulate warmth, use woolen
> mittens and hat, protect all of body with adequate rain gear;
>-remove layers to allow perspiration to evaporate during exercise;
>-add layers to preserve prewarmed air next to body as it cools; and
> remember that head, neck and groin areas are the most vulnerable;
> 30-35% of body heat can be lost through the head.

When appropriate, relax and eat high energy foods. The searchers must be adequately trained in survival techniques. We advise each participant to carry emergency bivouac gear for shelter (space blanket, garbage bags, and matches) construction. In an emergency, each member should be fully equipped to spend a night in the bush. Also, bivouac early to avoid exposure and exhaustion.

Some additional comments:
- If immersed in cold water DON'T drownproof, use Heat Escape Lessening Posture (HELP) to minimize heat loss;
- Be aware of the wind chill factor, 40 kmph:
  - -1 degree C. air temp. is the equivalent of -18 degree C. reading on skin surface. If clothes are wet, the effect is worse;
- Get enough sleep; avoid alcohol and tobacco as these make it harder for the body to adjust to the cold; and
- Be careful not to become dehydrated. An adult needs at least 7 litres of water a day. 25% of stamina is lost when an adult loses 2 litres of water.

Severe sunburn and windburns may be present both winter or summer. Always keep your head covered if at all possible with a wide brimmed hat. Take advantage of any shade. Be sure to use snowglasses in snow and ice conditions. The bright sun reflection of snow and ice can result in snowblindness.

Even minor injuries are potentially dangerous in the wilderness. Treat all cuts, sprains or bruises carefully, with antiseptic powder or wash with plain soap and water. Foot blisters can be very painful. The searcher should be aware of blisters between toes and on the heals of the foot. To forestall this condition, keep your socks dry even if it means stopping and drying them over an open fire every so often. This same method is followed to prevent frostbite of the feet. If blisters do form, do not puncture them; cover with antiseptic and apply a dressing.

SHOCK

Shock is a serious condition that is present in some degree with any injury resulting from a depressed state of many bodily functions. Shock can threaten life even though the initial injury itself is not life threatening.

The vital functions are depressed when there is a loss of blood volume, a reduced rate of blood flow, or an insufficient supply of oxygen in the blood. Injury related shock commonly referred to as traumatic shock is decidedly different from electric shock, insulin shock, and any of the other forms of "shock" such as anaphyleptic shock which will be discussed later.

Many things increase the severity of shock such as abnormal changes in body temperature, poor resistance of the victim to stress and pain, rough handling, or delay in treatment.

CAUSES

Shock may be caused by severe injuries of all types: bleeding, loss of plasma, loss of fluid other than blood, such as vomiting, internal bleeding, poisoning, alcohol or drug use. Shock can also be caused by obstruction of the airway or injury to the respiratory system.

SIGNS AND SYMPTOMS

Any or all of the following signs and symptoms may be present:
- paleness
- cold clammy skin
- sweating
- thirst
- nausea and vomiting
- anxiety
- change in the level of consciousness
- increase in pulse rate and a tendency to become weak
- shallow and rapid breathing

EARLY STAGES OF SHOCK

In the early stages of shock, the body compensates for a decreased blood flow by constricting the blood vessels in the skin, soft tissues, and skeletal muscles. This constriction raises an emergency effort by the body to re-distribute the flow of blood to the heart, brain and other vital internal organs, and may lead to the following signs: pale or bluish skin colour, cold to the touch; and moist and clammy skin. In the case of victims with dark skin pigmentation, it may be necessary to rely primarily on the colour of the mucous membranes on the inside of the mouth or under the eyelids or nail beds. The victim may be weak, have a rapid pulse, increased rate of breathing, restlessness, severe thirst, vomiting and quite possibly, thrash about.

LATER STAGES OF SHOCK

If the victim's condition deteriorates, he may become apathetic and relatively unresponsive. His eyes will be sunken with a vacant or blank expression and his pupils may be widely dilated. Some of the blood vessels in the skin may be congested, producing a mottled appearance. This is a sign that the victim's blood pressure has fallen to a dangerously low level. If left untreated, the victim will probably lose consciousness; his body temperature will drop and he may expire.

TREATMENT

Treatment can be expressed as attempting to:

        1) improve circulation of blood;
        2) ensure an adequate supply of oxygen; and
        3) maintain normal body temperature.

First, eliminate the cause of the shock. Keep the victim lying down and cover him with a blanket, sweater, jacket, or space blanket. If injuries of the neck and spine are suspected, do not move the victim until he is properly prepared for transportation unless it is necessary to protect him from further injury. An open airway is of prime concern and must be maintained regardless of his condition.

A victim in shock may improve with his feet raised. This position helps to improve blood flow from the lower extremities. However, should he experience difficulties in breathing after being placed in this position, lower his feet to the original position.

Keep the victim warm enough to overcome chilling. If he is exposed to cold or dampness, place blankets or additional clothing over and under him. Do not add extra heat because raising the surface temperature is harmful. Heat will draw blood back to the skin and thus away from the more vital organs within.

When time factors indicate that medical aid may be unavailable for some time, warm fluids may be administered depending on the cause of his injury. Fluids can not be administered for victims of internal bleeding, abdominal wounds or head injuries. Alcohol, since it tends to dilate blood vessels, is not a good substitute for warm drinks. Offer liquids only if victim is conscious.

Finally, a victim suffering from shock should never be left alone. He should be reassured about his condition and the steps being taken to ensure his well being. It is also advisable to place a victim in the recovery position.

CASUALTY HANDLING

How a casualty is handled once he has been found determines to some extent how both the casualty and his rescuers recover from the ordeal.

Casualty handling divides itself into five stages:

A. Approach
B. Assessment of injuries and priorities
C. Treatment
D. Lifting/Loading
E. Transport

APPROACH: A SEARCHER'S PERSPECTIVE

"A dead rescuer is not very helpful" or "Who needs a second patient?" Flippant, but true!

As you approach a casualty, check the environment so that you can avoid the same fate. Be on the lookout for such dangers as obstacles, falling trees, muskeg, live wires, or dangerous animals.

Constantly talk to the casualty as you approach. If he can hear, you, it will reassure him, and perhaps save you from being shot.

Decide on the safest approach to him and as you proceed; try to figure out the best way to move him out.

ASSESSMENT OF INJURIES AND PRIORITIES

As you assess your patient for injury, keep in mind the ABC's:

Airway: Is anything putting pressure on his body? ie. tie, fallen objects, or tight-fitting chest clothing. Is the head in a position to cut off his air passage? If he is unconscious, hyperextend the neck to allow free access of air. If the casualty is talking, why do you not need to check the airway?

Breathing: Look, listen, feel! Put your ear over his mouth and look for chest to rise, feel if air is moving against your cheek, and listen for the sounds of air passing. If no respiration, one person breathes 4 good breaths to get oxygen into lungs - re-inflate immediately and one breath every five seconds while the other continues assessing injuries.

Circulation: Use your eyes and hands. Keep checking as you run your hands over and under your patient, making sure there are no areas of heavy or life-threatening bleeding. If there are, treat as soon as possible with direct pressure where it is bleeding. Bind up tightly to stop the flow but not to stop all circulation below the dressing. The cleaner the material you cover a wound with the better, but remember, infection can be cured, bloodlessness cannot.

Now check for a pulse. Unless a person is an athlete, a rate of 60-100 a minute is no cause for alarm. But you can tell if it is weak, racing, "shocky" (too slow), or irregular. This could give you an idea of how immediate help is needed. If victim is hypothermic, there may be no pulse in extremities; check throat area for possible pulse.

Check for other injuries: breaks, bruising, penetrating wounds. Keep talking and asking questions. The onset of belligerence, restlessness, or lethargy can indicate a deteriorating condition.
Make certain to check the vertebrae in the neck and spine before letting the patient move or before you move him. Since a spinal injury can paralyse or even kill, why do you not check it before you work on airway and breathing?

TREATMENT

Treatment depends on the rescuers' previous knowledge, what he has with him in the way of first aid supplies, and ingenuity. That magazine you stuck in your packsack: Miss February and her pals make a great small splint. The patient's tie, handkerchief, belt, etc. can hold it in place. Saplings, long flashlight, ax handle...and best of all the 'splint' that the patient has with him at all times, the victim's other body parts. Shirt tails can make bandages and strappings. Use the patient's--you need to keep intact and warm to get him out.

Know what treatments the bush has to offer: Jewelweed juice or plantain for poison ivy; mud to poultice stings and bites; chewed up spruce inner bark for infections; wet moss to reduce swelling (weather permitting), or snow for the same purpose (but never directly against the skin).

MOVING THE PATIENT - LIFTING AND LOADING

Here is where the would-be rescuer can do himself (and his patient) irreparable harm. Doing yourself harm will not help the casualty, and can be extremely serious under bush rescue conditions. Self preservation is the key!

The Rescuer:

Remember, the larger the muscle used, the less strain and energy involved. Try holding up a heavy book with thumb and forefinger at arms length. Now try holding it up with hand and arm; hold it close in to your body. The second principle involved - the closer to your centre of gravity, the less effort involved. Third, try lifting something with your feet together, and with them comfortably apart and see which feels most stable. In short:

1. use the largest muscle groups;
2. lift as close to your body axis as possible;
3. lift from a broad base. "Prepare to lift...lift" (commands); and
4. for self preservation, try to keep your spine straight when lifting.

The Patient:

If the patient appears to have no spinal injuries, he can be blanket lifted onto an improvised stretcher; carried short distances with a blanket; shoulder dragged; pelvis carried; or various hand seats.

If the casualty has suspected back injury, he needs to be log-rolled onto a rigid surface like a back board with traction maintained to protect the spine.

A patient should be moved as smoothly as possible. The person at the patient's head calls the shots, eg. "Move on 3." He should also talk to and reassure the patient on a regular basis.

TRANSPORT

The patient should be positioned on whatever carrier device used in the position most comfortable to the patient and most stable for carrying. The casualty should be secured to the stretcher so that uneven terrain does not cause slipping and weight redistribution.

Preparing a blanket stretcher. For additional support, strap three separate belts across the ends and middle of the blanket.

IMPROVISED BLANKET STRETCHER

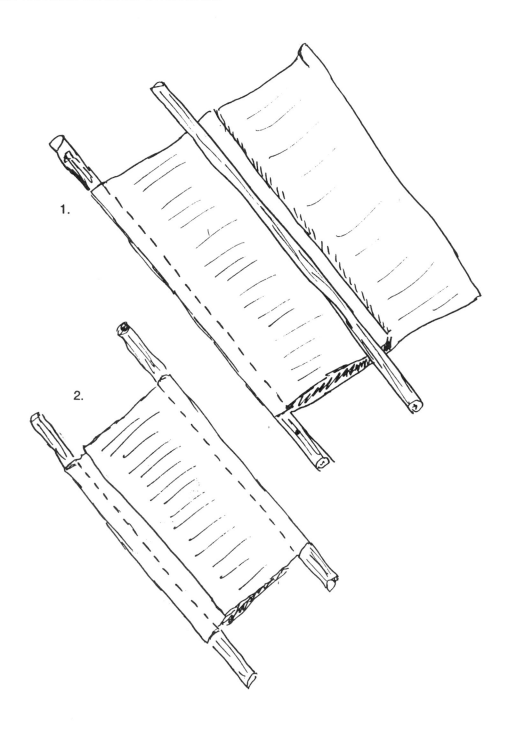

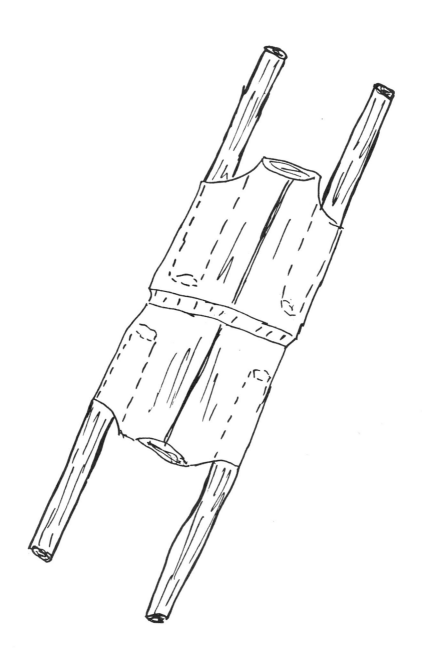

Portable stretchers, backboards, etc., are a solution, but what can you substitute if they are _not_ immediately available?

Emergency stretcher - use coats or blanket - make it longer than necessary to share the load. If impractical, use belt or rope for extra support (shoulder to pole). When transporting, use this suggested guide-line: Field - feet first; uphill - head first; downhill - feet first; heavy bush - feet first.

IMPROVISING A STRETCHER

BLANKET

When a victim has to be carried a great distance, it is advisable to improvise a stretcher. One technique is to cut down two saplings, approximately 2 1/2 metres in length. The poles should be at least 1/2 metre longer than the patient. If a blanket is available, lay it flat on the ground. Place one pole in the centre of the blanket. Fold blanket in half, Now place the second pole in centre. Finally, fold the free edge back over the second pole. For further support strap 3 separate belts at the ends and middle of the blanket.

Teamwork and communication are essential when transporting a stretcher case through dense forests.

COATS

The other method of improvising a stretcher does not require a blanket. A minimum of two coats are needed; three are more than sufficient. Once coats are removed, zipper or button up the fronts, placing the sleeves inside the coat itself. Run the poles through the sleeves.

If a patient is to be carried great distances, secure tump lines at each end of the stretcher. When possible, strap the victim into the stretcher. Always test the strength of the stretcher before attempting to transport a victim. To aid in the comfort of the patient while transporting, four bearers should commence walking with the leg closest to the stretcher. When lifting, one person should take charge.

Commands: 1. PREPARE TO LIFT
             2. LIFT

WATER LOSS EFFECT:

PERCENTAGE OF BODY WEIGHT

1-5%	6-10%	11-12%	
THIRST	HEADACHE	DELIRIUM	
VAGUE FEELING OF DISCOMFORT	DIZZINESS	SWOLLEN TONGUE	1 LITRE OF WATER = 1 kg
ECONOMY OF MOVEMENT	DRY MOUTH	TWITCHING	
IMPATIENCE	TINGLING IN LIMBS	DEAFNESS	
NO APPETITE	BLUE TINGE TO SKIN	DIM VISION	
FLUSHED SKIN	INDISTINCT	NUMB SKIN	2 CUPS OF WATER IS ROUGHLY = 1/2 kg
INCREASE IN PULSE RATE	LABOURED BREATHING	SHRIVELLED SKIN	
PULSE RATE	BREATHING	SKIN	
NAUSEA	INABILITY TO WALK	INABILITY TO SWALLOW	

THE EFFECTS LISTED ARE THOSE EXPERIENCED WHEN THE WATER LOSS IS WITHIN THE LOWER LIMITS BASED ON THE WORK OF DR. E. F. ADOLPH, WHO STUDIED THE EFFECTS OF WATER LOSS ON MEN IN THE DESERT.

GETTING BUGGED

Come spring and summer, many people head to the wilderness or for the cottage. Some canoe; others camp and hike. However, all will soon meet up with black flies, mosquitos, deer flies, hornets, wasps and bees. Even with nets and repellents, it is still a bothersome time of year.

Considering that in Ontario, there are over forty species of mosquitos and at least fifty species of black flies, an individual stranded in the wilderness, especially during springtime, is faced with the maddening problem of remaining sane while swarms of bugs continually harass him! Fortunately, not all species attack man. While the female mosquitoes (males don't bite) converge at night, black flies attack only during daylight hours.

It may be of interest to note that mosquitos breed in stagnant water; black flies need running or white waters.

Insects are attracted to warm blooded beings, especially to people, by scent; they prefer fair-skinned morsels over individuals with darker complexions. Perspiration, dark clothing (navy blue, red, and plaids) and sweet smells act as magnets to Mr. Bug!

With a tent, commercial netting and repellent, one does have some relief. Without these, you are at the mercy of a scourge that gives no relief and has made the strong, weak. To prevent a tragedy as well as to cope with the bugs, start early to prepare

Cover all exposed skin with mud to ward off the ever-present mosquitos and blackflies.

for them. Stop eating bananas and switch to citrus fruits. Bananas release an odor through the skin that actually attracts some insects; oranges, chamomile and mint teas do the opposite. So does garlic! Brightly coloured clothing (red, blue, orange, yellow) attract; neutral colours (beige, light green, white, brown) tend to give some relief.

Since insects are attracted by sweet scents, common sense dictates that the first thing to do in order to repel them is avoiding perfume, lotions, scented soaps or detergents when washing. Use unscented soaps if you must, or, when washing your clothing, rinse in several changes of water.

Also, walk at a slower pace. This tends to reduce the level of perspiration. Layer your clothing using loose, neutral coloured garments to cover as much exposed skin as possible. Wear loosely-fitting garments, and seal shirt cuffs, collars, and trousers (stick into socks), thereby preventing Mr. Fly from gaining entry. Wear gloves.

If you become separated from your tent, net or repellent, you will have to tough it out. Erect your shelter in a clearing; windy, sunny, and bright areas may afford some relief. Keep in mind that insects are hyper on cloudy, calm days. Sit or sleep near a smoky fire; it will keep the bugs away. Smear mud (or, if available, coal oil) over all exposed parts of your body and cover up everywhere. Soothe bites with crushed plantain and yarrow leaves. A dip in the lake will also do wonders to reduce swelling and itching. Don't give those pesky critters the opportunity of getting you.

More preventative medicine:

1.   Pennyroyal teas, if consumed in large quantities, also repel insects.

2.   Inside your shelter, keep a punky, smoky fire going. In most cases, smoke drives bugs away.

3.   Erect shelters in clearings, where every breeze could be felt. Sunny, bright, and windy areas reduce insects' activities; conversely, insects are hyper on cloudy, calm days.

4.   If everything else fails, cover every exposed part of your body with mud.

No shelter can ever be completely bug-proofed. All the survivor can do on those hot muggy nights is to construct punky fires inside his shelter to ward off the swarms of mosquitoes. Attempting to seal off entrance-ways with boughs, plastic, or tarps simply does not work; the bugs will somehow get in. All the victim can do is cover all exposed parts, placing some clothing over his face, and bear the maddening noise created by the unending swarms of insects.

With regards to first aid treatment for insect bites, there is very little the survivor can do. Besides covering up to protect himself from other bites, we have found the following remedies to be most effective for mosquito and black fly bites:

1.   Do not scratch, since this only aggravates the situation. If possible, enjoy a brief swim in a cool lake. Cold water, besides cleaning your skin (and disinfecting the bites), soothes itchy skin. After a swim, the urge to scratch diminishes considerably.
2.   Liberally cover bites with the juice of jewelweed. In extreme cases, we first boiled the juice. This resulted in a thick paste which we applied to badly infected areas.
3.   Place a compress of crushed Plantain, Yarrow, or St. John's Wort leaves directly over bitten areas. Change this poultice on a regular basis, that is, three or four times daily.
4.   As a last resort, apply cold mud on badly infected bites. This temporarily relieves the itching, later, thoroughly wash and apply any available poultice.

In the case of bees, wasps, and hornets, many people are surprised to learn that milligram for milligram, the venom of a bee is more powerful than that of a cobra.

More people die from bee and wasp stings than from snake bites. If a person is sensitive to stings, he may go into anaphylactic shock.

When stung, carefully remove the stinger with a clean object. Do so in a sideways motion. Otherwise, pulling it straight out will inject the remaining venom into the skin. Clean and elevate the infected area, and rest.

As a preventative measure, bees and hornets are more active, and therefore more likely to be bothersome, on bright, warm sunny days and immediately following heavy rains. Furthermore, they are attracted by sweet scents such as perfume and deodorants; brightly coloured clothing; freshly killed game or bloody carcasses; and free-flowing wounds and cuts.

The survivor is advised to keep his site clean. Any butchering should be done away from the living area. Also, no one should swat at bees and hornets or disturb their nests.

SANITATION

Outside of the normal facilities set up for sanitation in an emergency situation, a woman's anatomy has other requirements. There is the problem of menstrual fluid as well as that of daily vaginal discharge. The most important thing to remember in preventing complications is to keep the area as dry as possible.

Menstrual fluid can be absorbed in a makeshift pad made of a sleeve or another piece of rectangular cloth stuffed with moss. The moss can be thrown out and the sleeve rinsed out for further use.

Vaginitis is a yeast infection caused by a yeast, normally found in the vagina, getting the chance to grow out of control. The conditions conclusive to this are high heat (a normal condition for this area) and moisture (a preventable condition). The infection is characterized by a frothy white discharge and itch. Complications can arise when the skin around the vagina becomes infected by scratching. The only way to clear up the infection is with a doctor's prescription for a fungicide suppository. Prevention is far easier, by changing pants or at least a padding or by allowing the area to be uncovered, the vaginal area can be kept dry. Padding can be made from any spare square of cloth, sleeve, cuff, pocket or pocket lining from pants or shirt but it should be made of an absorbent cloth such as cotton, wool or rayon. Warning: nylon and polyester are not absorbent and underwear made of these fabrics exclusively (ie. without a cotton crotch) can lead to vaginitis, wilderness situation or not.

If weather permits, keeping the area free of clothing will allow evaporation to take place. A system of tunic and leggings, if the materials are available will keep the vaginal area dry and the body warm.

Infection from ecoli bacteria is also possible. This is characterized by a brownish discharge, more frightening than dangerous. It is caused by the ecoli bacteria normally found in the intestine becoming established in the vagina. Again, a doctor's prescription is needed to clear it up but this infection can be easily prevented by wiping to the back. This is especially important in a wilderness situation when washing is difficult and diarrhea inevitable.

Rashes similar to diaper rash and heat rash are also possible. Again, the solution is to keep the area as dry as possible. If there is any Vaseline in your first aid kit, it will provide some extra protection from moisture and protect the affected tissues from friction against clothing.

In conclusion, prevention is far easier than treatment in a wilderness situation. Keeping the vaginal area dry and as clean as possible can provide at least a measure of comfort for women in this situation.

SOME COMMENTS ON FIELD SANITATION

The main problem is one of being unfamiliar with the situation; for example, people feel "unclean" when having a bowel movement in the bush. Some precautions make this task less dreadful:

1.   dig a shallow latrine away from camp;

2.   when finished, cover the feces with dirt (or else maggots may appear); and

3.   to prevent ecoli infection (from feces infection) wipe to the back. If toilet paper is not available, moss may be used.

If you have diarrhea, don't worry; it will eventually clear itself up. Stay put!

It is important to keep dry or a rash similar to diaper rash will develop.

To prevent any discomfort, always wear loose clothing made of cotton or wool and stay dry.

A BRIEF SUMMARY OF FIRST AID TECHNIQUES

ARTIFICIAL RESPIRATION

Watch victim's chest. Lay on back and wipe any foreign object out of mouth with fingers. Place one hand under neck and lift. Tilt head back by holding top of head with your other hand. Pinch nostrils and place your mouth over the victim's mouth and blow four quick breaths. Remove your mouth and watch chest to see if it rises and falls. If victim isn't breathing, check again for foreign objects in the mouth. Tilt head back and repeat direct mouth to mouth respiration. If still not breathing, turn victim on his side and give four sharp slaps between shoulder blades to remove any foreign objects. Check again for foreign objects. Tilt head back once more and apply direct artificial respiration.

BLEEDING

Stop bleeding by pressing a sterile gauze dressing or any clean cloth over wound with your hand. If gauze is soaked with blood, put more on top of first covering. We advise against the random use of tourniquets. When bleeding has stopped wrap the dressings in place.

BROKEN BONES

Keep patient warm. If bone breaks skin, stop the bleeding with dressings. Use splints to stop any movement of fracture, using any material at hand. This includes birch bark and branches. Splints should be long enough to go past joint above and below break...too long is better than too short. If bleeding is present, elevate bleeding area. However, if back or neck is broken, do not move victim but keep him warm. Get help immediately.

HEAD INJURY

Often, the symptoms are dizziness, bleeding in ears and nose. Lay victim down and keep warm. Don't allow patient to sit or walk. Do not attempt to block ears. Get help immediately.

UNCONSCIOUSNESS - REASON UNKNOWN

Search pockets, wallet, body, for medical alert cards or bracelets. If victim is not breathing, give artificial respiration. If face is red, raise head slightly; if face is pale, lower head. If victim vomits, roll on side to keep them from choking on vomit. Place in recovery position until help arrives. Even though he's unconscious, the victim may be able to hear you. Talk to him in a soothing and comforting voice.

DEALING WITH DEATH

A person in your party died of overexposure! While attempting to cross a frozen lake, the thin ice gave way. By the time your party arrived, the blue corpse was a mass of solid flesh. Upon pulling the body out of the water, you covered it with a blanket. All other members of the group were asked to write down as many details of the accident as possible, since an inquest is bound to take place. Two people were directed to summon help!

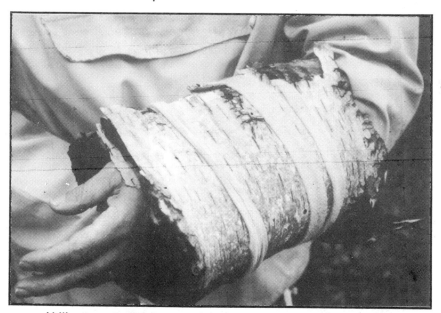

Utilize any available material to secure a broken bone. In an emergency, Birch bark makes an excellent splint. Pad inside of splint with soft, dry moss.

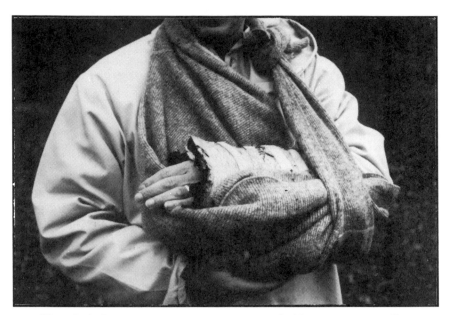
The victim's own sweater serves as a suitable emergency sling.

Should some people lapse into shock, gently comfort them with a soothing voice. How did the accident occur? If the victim's death was his fault, then say so! Placing the blame for errors where it belongs may save some other person's life.

Once help arrives, you are faced with the awesome task of explaining the accident to the authorities and, in some cases, to the victim's family. There is no easy way to tell a parent (or other family members) that a relative has been found dead! It is a nightmare to the person hearing the news.

Generally speaking, this is not the role of the group leader, but falls within the jurisdiction of the police, who are specially trained to perform this touchy task. However, it may be necessary for some of you to perform this unenviable task. Should the need arise, it is imperative that the case be handled with tact and compassion and, if possible, have a neighbour or friend present.

While the family bears the brunt of tremendous shock and sorrow, it is you, the bearer of bad news, who often feels this same pain and sorrow, especially if the deceased was a personal friend or a member of your group.

At this stage, family members may wish somebody on which to lean, like a rabbi, a minister, or a priest, who may help to alleviate the grief and frustration usually felt by the family. Perhaps there is no way to adequately prepare a family for the news of death. As one police officer claimed, each case must be approached with "professional detachment".

"Certainly you are emotionally involved. You think about the experience afterward. It's not as if you feel the same as they do, but you do sense what they feel."

This is a most difficult duty. In effect, you are telling someone their loved one is not coming home - ever again; and, while the family is left to mourn and share its sorrow, the bearer of bad news should leave.

VERY BRIEF OVERVIEW OF EMERGENCY FIRST AID

Approaching the Victim

> A. Don't panic - be calm - forget blood and screaming
> B. Survey total picture - take charge
> C. Identify yourself and tell victim not to move
> D. Remember your priorities.

PRIORITIES

Diagnosis	Priority	Treatment
HISTORY OF ACCIDENT OBSERVATION hear, see, feel pulse observe surroundings	1. prevent further injury 2. breathing 3. circulation 4. bleeding 5. unconsciousness	* remove A.R. CPR (if known) RED rule usually recovery position maintain airway

*treatment of the priorities should be nearly simultaneous, including a spinal check

If talking, the victim is breathing, circulation and conscious; ask about:
> a. poisoning
> b. burns
> c. fractures

Reassure the victim constantly - talk to him. Get medical aid.

Artificial Respiration (A.R.)
-check to make sure victim is not only sleeping.

Method	Procedure	Rates
<u>Mouth to Mouth</u> and alternates; worry about obstructions only if they cause a problem.	1. Hypertension to clear airway. 2. Seal nose if necessary. 3. Mouth seal. 4. Quick blows to start then continue making sure chest is rising and falling. 5. Adult rhythm should be: Blow 1,2,3,4 Blow...	Adult 1/5 sec.; forceful. Child 1/3 sec.; less forceful. Infant 1/2 sec. puffs only that would fill your cheeks. Support an infant's back.
<u>Sylvester</u>	1. On back (victim). 2. Extend neck and keep airway clear. 3. Arms on chest, side by side. 4. On knees at head (rescuer). 5. Press on victim's hands to count of 1 and 2. 6. Pull hands up like rowing count of 3 and 4 and back for 5 (adult rate).	Adult 1/5 sec. Child 1/3 sec. Infant 1/2 sec.
<u>Holger-Neilson</u>	1. On stomach, hands under head. 2. Extend neck and keep airway clear. 3. Thumbs on middle of shoulder blades. 4. Press 3,4 up while lifting his arms. Back for 5. (adult rate) 5. Don't drop arms. Keep smooth rhythm.	Same as Sylvester

A. BLEEDING - get a tetanus shot before you go on long trips.

Treatment   <u>R</u>- est
                 <u>E</u>- levation
                 <u>D</u>- direct pressure

1. Internal Bleeding

Diagnosis-	Treatment
T-thirst	1. raise legs
A-air hunger	2. rest
R-restlessness	3. nothing by mouth unless far from help
	- then only sips of water
	4. warmth and reassurance
	5. medical aid

2. Sucking Chest Wound Treatment

1. Seal hole with hand, then plastic.
2. Secure seal.
3. Lay injured side down.

3. Eye Injuries

1. Always cover both eyes.
2. Gauze or cup over injury without pressure.
3. Secure bandages in place.

4. Bandaging

1. Use a sterile dressing.
2. Use porous materials.
3. Use a ring pad for foreign bodies.
4. Never remove bandages, only add more (if it won't stop bleeding).
5. No tourniquets unless limb is in danger.

B. FRACTURES (including sprains and dislocations)

Open fractures should be covered with gauze, bandaged with a ring bandage and generally treated like other fractures after the bleeding has been dealt with.

Diagnosis	Treatments (General Rules)
Pain	1. Treat in place and position you find it in.
Swelling	2. Immobilize - splint in one way or another.
Discoloration	3. Steady and support - sling and/or bandage.
Tenderness	4. Keep warm.
Loss of power	5. Keep lying down if possible.
Deformity	6. Have a purpose behind any movements you make.

Don't: 1. Set bones
            2. Relocate dislocations
            3. Move victim or part of him unnecessarily

SPLINTS

1. cover whole fracture
2. cover 2 joints
3. are stiff enough   - CHECK PULSE BELOW ANY SPLINT
4. are wide enough
5. are padded where needed

SPECIFICS

Skull - don't probe or clean serious wounds - cover to prevent infection; do not seal ears - ensure for drainage.
Jaw - let him continue to hold it
Ribs - no tape
Arms - splints covering 2 joints etc. then a sling
Collarbone - body splint and sling
Legs - splint etc. and elevate leg
Ankle - if in a boot leave it there but only leave one lace in at top

Spinal or Suspected Spinal Injury

(i) help less than 45 minutes away   - don't move him
                                        - immobilize and steady without moving
                                          parts
                                        - assure him and wait for help

(ii) help a long way off   - use of a cervical collar and backboard
                                          if you have the training.

COLD

Problem	Diagnosis	Prevention	Treatment
Frostnip	skin white and waxy	buddy system - no rubbing	gentle warmth using skin to skin
Frostbite	same as above but stays white when pressed	buddy system	leave frozen and get to hospital or if you thaw it do not stop as you have a stretcher case now
Hypothermia	shivering, violent shiver, muscular impairment, sluggishness in all areas, no shivering, victim loses grip on things, unconsciousness, death	1.buddy system 2.recognize signs 3.prepare for weather 4.eat 5.Prevent dehydration 6.watch effect of wind and water	1. immediate recognition 2.shelter and warm clothes 3. warm - hot water immersion with with extremities hanging out or - in a sleeping bag with others (nude) - warm fluids if conscious 4. get to medical aid

In Hypothermia, the body core will cool for up to 2 hours after reheating has started so recognition and treatment must be prompt.

SUMMARY

Learn the basic and general rules of First Aid and combine this with common sense to deal with all specific situations.

EXAMPLE OF A FIRST AID KIT

Triangular bandages (2)
Roll of adhesive tape (tri cut)
Strong cord (splint tying material)
   - shoe laces
Bandaids or equivalent
Scissors or knife
field dressings

sterile gauze (4 X 4 pads)
piece of plastic or space blanket
small notebook and pencil
safety pins
green soap
tylenol
roller gauze

SUGGESTED READING

Angier, B. *Being Your own Wilderness Doctor*. Harrisburg: Stackpole Books, 1968.

Arnold, R.E., M.D. *What to Do About Bites & Stings of Venomous Animals*, New York: Collier Books, 1973.

Donaghy, R. & D. *Wilderness Emergency Care*. Rexdale: Humber College Press, 1980.

Edholm, O.G. and A.L. Bacharach. *The Physiology of Human Survival*. Academic Press, 1965.

Farmer, K. *Woman In The Woods*. Harrisburg: Stackpole Books, 1976.

Folk, G.E. *Textbook of Environmental Physiology.* Philadelphia: Lea and Febriger, 1966.

Forgey, Wm. W. *Wilderness Medicine*. Pittsboro, Indiana: Indiana Camp Supply Books, 1979.

Lathrop, T.G., M.D. *Hypothermia, Killer of the Unprepared*. The Mazamas, 1970.

Tabor, J. "Layering: The Inside Story." *Backpacker*, Aug./Sept. 1981.

Washburn, B. "Frostbite." *New England Journal of Medicine*, 266: 974-989.

West, A. and Smallman, B. *Goodbye Bugs*! Toronto: Grosvenor House Press, 1983.

Werner, David. *Where There Is No Doctor*. Palo Alto: Hesperian Foundation, 1977.

Wilderson, J. *Medicine For Mountaineering*. Seattle: 2nd Edition, 1975.

APPENDIX

HUMBER COLLEGE, NORTH CAMPUS, REXDALE, CANADA

WILDERNESS SURVIVAL PROGRAMME

COURSE OUTLINE

SESSION I

Introduction:

(a)   Getting to know each other - gear required; our expectation of all students

(b)   Survival hints
- don't panic
- remain stationary
- natural shelter   ) see Chart; Case Studies
- keep emergency kit in vehicle)

(c)   Essentials for survival: developing a survival mentality
- shelter   - fire
- food   - water

(d)   Shelters
- lean-to   - canoe)   Complete on Session II
- tarp   - poncho)
- natural

(e)   Survival simulation - Film (optional)

(f)   Edible plants (assignments)

(g)   Required reading

SESSION II

(a)   Fire and its construction
- charred cloth   - flint
- flashlight and others   - flint stick
- squaw-wood   - Basswood and willow (location)

(b)   Hypothetical situations

(c)   Finding direction

(d)   Predicting weather

(e)   Basics in first-aid
     i) A.R.   iii) broken bones
     ii) cuts   iv) summary

(f)   Shelters (continue)

(g)   Kudlik

(h)   Edible plants

SESSION III

(a)   Edible plants (assignments)

(b)   Hypothetical situations

(c)   Preparation for trip #1 (maps, gear needed)

(d)   The car as a survival device

(e)   Snowshoeing (Winter)

(f)   Jerky making

(g)   Figure 4 deadfall

SESSION IV

(a)   More edible plants plus bannock and pemmican - (flour - raisins - jerky - fat - cup, board)

(b)   Outdoor sanitation

(c)   Keeping bugs away (Spring) - (mud, oranges, chamomile, pennyroyal, bananas, clothing, soap, perfume)

(d)   Emergency signals

(e)   Preparation for trip #1

(f)   Trail blazing

WEEKEND TRIP #1

SESSION V

(a)   Review trip #1 -
       - comments, questionnaire - examine slides taken
       - review work done to date

(b)   Construction of fire bow - (heavy string, bow, spindle)

(c)   Food cooking techniques - rock, pit

SESSION VI

(a)   Plucking birds

(b)   Skinning animals

(c)   Filleting fish

(d)   Preparation for trip #2

(e)   Field cooking techniques - (in valley, following skinning)

SESSION VII

(a)   Snares and deadfalls   - saplings
                              - wire
                              - string

(b)   Shelters (stone, variations)

(c)   Hide tanning   - rabbit from previous week
                              - frame

(d)   Carbide, potassium permanganate and sugar (additional firestarting techniques)

SESSION VIII

(a)   Survival tools to make

- spear	- hooks
- harpoons	- tri-stand
- drying racks	

(b)   Throwing stick

(c)   Preparation for weekend trip #2

WEEKEND TRIP #2

SESSION IX

(a)   Review trip #2, examine slides taken

(b)   Guest speaker - survival mentality

(c)   Review work done to date

(d)   Basic orienteering (time permitting), field & bush navigation

SESSION X

(a)   Questions, answers, sharing skills and resources

(b)   Pursue special interests and concerns

(c)   Finish any incomplete sections, assignments

(d)   Course evaluation. Certificates

(e)   Leathercraft (time permitting)

(f)   Guest speaker: survivor

Constructing a smoking rack.

HYPOTHETICAL SITUATIONS: DISCUSSED IN CLASS

1. HOLOCAUST

A disastrous holocaust has occurred. Surviving remnants of humankind are now scattered across the world. You are the leader of one such group consisting of four (4) men, five (5) women, three (3) children - a total of twelve (12).

Habitat: A small island seven (7) by twenty (20) kilometers. You have weapons. Distance from the mainland is ten (10) kilometers.

One day, your group notices a flotilla of six (6) canoes approaching the island.

Discuss your course(s) of action.

Season: Optional.

Note: Civilization as we now know it is non-existent.

2. LUGGAGE PACKING

DESCRIPTION

You will spend the month of July in Alaska. On your flight you can carry 20 kg. of luggage.

Familiarize yourself with the climatic conditions of Alaska.
From the list below decide the particular articles which you feel will be essential to take. More than one of each article may be taken. Do not exceed 20 kg.

ARTICLES

Suitcase	- 1.0 kg.	Trunk	- 3.0 kg.
Flight bag	- .5 kg.	Sweater	- .7 kg.
Dress	- .3 kg.	Coat	- 1.0 kg.
Suit	- 1.0 kg.	Skirt	- .4 kg.
Blouse or Shirt	- .2 kg.	Shorts	- .1 kg.
Pants or Jeans	- .2 kg.	Underwear	- .1 kg.
Purse	- .2 kg.	Toiletries	- .4 kg.
Cosmetics	- .4 kg.	Sunglasses	- .1 kg.
Camera	- .4 kg.	Books	- .5 kg.
Travel Clock	- .1 kg.	Radio	- 1.0 kg.
Travelling Iron	- .4 kg.	Map	- .1 kg.
Umbrella	- .2 kg.	Swimming Suit	- .1 kg
Raincoat	- .3 kg.	Jewellery	- .1 kg.
Skis and Poles	- 2.0 kg.	Ski Boots	- 2.0 kg.
Games	- .4 kg.	Rubbers	- 1.0 kg.
Parka	- 1.0 kg.	Snow Boots	- 1.5 kg.
Towel	- .5 kg.		

First   A) Individual decision

Second   B) Group discussion. Please come to a concensus.

3. A QUESTION OF SURVIVAL

You are a crew member of a small cargo plane that has crash-landed in the MacKenzie River Delta. Your last chartered position placed you some 200 km south of Aklavik. You are off-course, therefore there is no hope of rescue. You must travel to the nearest point of civilization (Aklavik). Your task is to decide which items you need to take in order to survive the journey. However, there are 21 items and the group (4 members) can only take 8. Season: Winter!!!

You must arrive at a group concensus of which 8 items you wish to take.

ITEMS

1. First-Aid kit	12. Stellar chart of area
2. Compass	13. Canteen
3. Inflatable life raft	14. Food rations
4. Flare pistol and 3 flares	15. One case of beer
5. Matches	16. Fish line and hooks
6. One case of pet milk	17. Extra parkas
7. 3 dozen chocolate bars	18. Snowshoes
8. Tent	19. Sleeping bags
9. Radio receiver (no transmitter)	20. Blankets
10. .45 Calibre pistol	21. Knapsacks
11. Knife	22. Bullets for pistol

4. ECOLOGY

A Bush Pilot is a conservationist and he is stranded in the Ontario Wilderness. He has a gun and some ammunition. Rank the following animals and birds in the order in which the Bush Pilot would hunt them in order that he might survive.

Snake	Fox	Rabbit	Wolf
Frog	Fawn	Bear	Canada Goose
Fish	Duck	Skunk	Porcupine
Crayfish	Ground Hog	Moose	Beaver

Remember to take the following into consideration when you are ranking the animals:

1. Food or lack of it

2. Danger of animal to the Pilot

3. Care for endangered species

4. Sportsmanship

5. Nature's way of housekeeping

5. A WORLD-WIDE TRAGEDY HAS OCCURRED

You are leaving urban society. There are ten (10) in the group. Time is of the essence.

The group could be gone for a week or for a decade.

List all of the articles you would consider taking.

Space (transportation) is at a premium. Don't forget: Time is of the essence.
Season: Your choice.

6. THE DOWNED AIRPLANE

i) SCENARIO

You were on a flight, from Thunder Bay to Fort Albany on James Bay, in a Dakota aircraft with a crew of two and six passengers.

During the flight, icing was encountered and finally the aircraft lost an engine and was forced to land in dense forest approximately 25 km southwest of a large lake. After surveying the crash site, you determined the aircraft would be invisible from the air due to the trees hiding it from view.

Before the crash you could see that the area was uninhabited; trees stretched for kilometres in all directions; and that the lake ahead, as shown on the map, would be the only large open area.

During the crash landing, all radio communications were lost due to broken equipment, and contrary to regulations, the aircraft did not carry a Crash Position Indicator.

In your opinion, the best bet for survival in the cold (-20°C) weather and deep snow-covered ground, is to get to the lake where you can visually signal search aircraft and where ski-equipped aircraft or helicopters can pick you up.

As no one was injured and it is only midday, everyone agrees to head for the lake as soon as possible.

Among the equipment and supplies in the aircraft available for your survival are the items listed.

Of immediate concern is the relative importance of each of the items to your survival.

Your task is to rank these items in order of importance so that you can safely reach the lake and survive until spotted by a search plane.

Place a 1 beside the most important item; a 2 beside the second most important, and so on.

ii) INSTRUCTIONS

This is an exercise in group decision making. Your group is to reach a group concensus. This means that the selection of each item must be agreed upon by each group member before it becomes part of a group decision. Concensus is difficult to reach; therefore, not every ranking will meet with everyone's approval. Try, as a group, to make each ranking one with which all group members can at least partially agree. The following are some guides to use in reaching concensus:

(1) Avoid arguing for your own individual judgement. Approach the task on the basis of logic.

(2) Avoid changing your mind only in order to reach agreement and avoid conflict. Support only solutions with which you are able to agree, somewhat at least.

(3) Avoid "conflict reducing" techniques such as majority vote, averaging or trading, in reaching your decision.

(4) View differences of opinion as helpful rather than as a hindrance in decision making.

Available equipment:

_____	matches
_____	case of dried fruit
_____	50 metres nylon rope
_____	20 metres nylon rope
_____	parachutes
_____	sleeping bags
_____	3 axes
_____	1-30-30 cal. rifle
_____	2 - .38 cal. pistols
_____	5 litres of water
_____	2 cases of tin food
_____	2 portable heating units
_____	folio of maps
_____	case of dried meat
_____	small packsack of cooking utensils
_____	magnetic compass
_____	signal flares
_____	First Aid kit
_____	fishing equipment
_____	snowshoes
_____	1 m toboggan

Your group task is to rank these items in order of importance to your survival.

WILDERNESS SURVIVAL COURSE

You are asked to complete and return this questionnaire within thirty (30) minutes. Your candid comments, constructive criticisms, and general opinions are needed to perfect our survival courses.

1.   Were you suitably prepared for both weekend outings? Explain.

2.   Were these outings too physically and/or mentally demanding? Not demanding enough?

3.   At this point, how confident are you in the bush?

4.   Was the area chosen suitable for a wilderness survival experience?

5.   Given this type of environment, what have you learned about yourself? Others?

6.   Was your interest in the bush stimulated (or the opposite) by the course? Explain. Please continue on next page...a detailed answer would be appreciated.

7.   Would you recommend this survival course to others? Explain.

8.   Why did you take this survival course?

9.   Are you planning to further your knowledge of wilderness survival skills? How?

10.   Did you take in less equipment and less food on the second outing? Explain.

11.   Was the procedure on animal (fish, bird and rabbit) preparation sufficient? Explain.

12.   Additional comments and suggestions.

STATISTICAL ANALYSES OF WILDERNESS SURVIVAL VICTIMS

A. INITIAL SURVEY - WILDERNESS SURVIVORS

704 cases: Province of Ontario: randomly selected.
1978 - 1987
704 = 100%

298 - lost 10 hrs. or less (day time)	42.3%	
175 - overnight	24.8%	623 cases or 88.4%
150 - 2 to 3 days	21.3%	
46 - 4 to 7 days	6.5%	
29 - 8 to 13 days	4.1%	81 cases or 11.6%
6 - 14 and/or more days	.85%	

Of these, 156 cases (21.88%) were professional outdoorsmen (guides, lumberjacks, trappers, etc.)

Remainder (548 or 78.12%) were novices from large urban centres.

B. SYNOPSIS: DURATION OF LOST INDIVIDUALS - PERCENTILE

YEAR	DAYS & PERCENTAGES					CASES
	1	2	3	4	4+ DAYS	
1975	66.8%	-	-	-	13.2%	15
1980	67.9%	22.7%	4.5%	0	4.5%	22
1981	93.8%	-	-	-	5.2%	19
1982	100.0%	-	-	-	-	20
						TOTAL 76

LOST:	1 DAY	-63 or	87.0%
	2 DAYS	- 5 or	6.5%
	3 DAYS	- 1 or	1.3%
	4 DAYS	- 0 or	0%
	4+ DAYS	- 4 or	5.2%

DATA COURTESY LAKEHEAD SEARCH & RESCUE UNIT
FINAL STATISTICS - G. FERRI, WINTER 1984

C. NORTHWEST ONTARIO: SEARCH & RESCUE CASES (L.S.& R. U.) - SUMMARY

YEAR	TOTAL CASES	SEASONS:				SUBJECTS:				
		W	SP	SU	FA	1	2	3	4	
1975	15	0	2	4	9	n/a	n/a	n/a	n/a	
1980	22	4	2	9	7	9	9	3	1	
1981	19	2	1	5	11	14	3	2	0	
1982	20	5	2	6	7	8	9	1	2	
TOTALS:	76	11	7	24	34	31	21	6	3	(TOTAL =61)
%:	100	15	9	31	45	49.6	33.6	10.4	5.2	(61 = 100%)

RAW DATA - COURTESY LAKEHEAD SEARCH & RESCUE UNIT
FINAL STATISTICS COMPILED BY G. FERRI, 1984.

1. O.P.P. Search and Rescue Occurrences
O.P.P. Jurisdiction *1978-1982

Year	S and R Occurrences	Hunters Patrons Fishermen, Trappers
1978	440	n/a
1979	446	n/a
1980	421	123
1981	330	135
1982	392	160
TOTAL 5 years	2,029	418

* All Districts

2. O.P.P. Search and Rescue Occurrences
Districts 12 to 17*
1978-1982

Year	S and R Occurrences	Hunters Patrons Fishermen, Trappers
1978	n/a	n/a
1979	n/a	n/a
1980	182	97
1981	121	107
1982	180	115

* where environment would be akin to wilderness conditions

3. O.P.P. SEARCH AND RESCUE OCCURRENCES BY SPECIFIC TYPE OF PERSON/PARTY LOST BY COMBINED O.P.P. DISTRICTS 12 TO 17, 1980-82

Year	Hunters	Patrons	Fishermen	Trappers	Total
1980	58	-	37	2	97
1981	61	3	36	7	107
1982	64	8	33	10	115
TOTAL (3 yrs)	183	11	106	19	319

4. O.P.P. SEARCH AND RESCUE OCCURRENCES BY SPECIFIC TYPE OF PERSON/PARTY LOST BY O.P.P. DISTRICTS 12 TO 17, AND COMPARED WITH ONTARIO TOTALS, 1982

District	Hunters	Patrons	Fishermen	Trappers	Total
12	12	1	1	-	14
13	12	7	6	-	25
14	14	-	13	3	30
15	7	-	3	4	14
16	10	1	5	1	16
17	9	-	5	2	16
Total Raw %	64 55.7%	8 7.0%	33 28.7%	10 8.7%	115 100%
Ontario %	88 72.7%	18 44.4%	44 75.0%	10 100.0%	160 71.9%

5. NUMBER OF PERSONS SEARCHED FOR BY SPECIFIC TYPE OF PERSON/PARTY LOST BY O.P.P. DISTRICTS 12 TO 17, 1982

Type of Party

District	Hunters	Patrons	Fishermen	Trappers	Total
12	17	2	1	-	20
13	14	9	7	-	30
14	20	-	20	4	44
15	11	-	4	4	19
16	12	-	12	2	26
17	11	-	6	2	19
TOTAL	85	11	50	12	158

6. SIZE OF PARTY SEARCH FOR (FREQUENCY DISTRIBUTION) BY SPECIFIC TYPE OF PERSON/PARTY LOST FOR O.P.P. DISTRICTS 12 TO 17, 1982

Type of Party

Party Size	Hunters	Patrons	Fishermen	Trappers	Total
1	43	5	20	8	76
2	19	3	8	2	32
3	2	-	5	-	7
4	-	-	-	-	-
5	-	-	-	-	-
TOTAL	64	8	33	10	115

CASE STUDIES...TO BE DISCUSSED

When reading the following accounts, these questions should be going through your mind:

1.   In what state of mind were the survivors?

2.   Did the wilderness play havoc with their mental health? How? Why?

3.   How did some of these individuals overcome this fear ? Why did others succumb to it?

4.   Why is man so afraid of the dark? How is this fear magnified in the bush? What is "bush fever"?

5.   Some measures taken seem extremely drastic. For example, cannibalism was practiced. Who should 'judge' the survivors? Why?

6.   What practical information did you learn from these case studies?

CASE STUDY A: RATIONAL VICTIM

Peter Fowler, 37 of Oakville, was flying alone to Winnipeg via Thunder Bay when his Beechcraft Bonanza went down eight kilometres off Western Duck Island south of Manitoulin Island.

Fowler said he had just seconds to inflate a rubber dinghy and get himself and his survival kit aboard before the plane was swamped by 2 m waves. He said it took two hours to drift to the unfortunately uninhabited island. He "wasn't too comfy" but built a lean-to and wrapped himself in a space blanket. "I dried my clothes and curled up and went to sleep until 7 a.m. After the fire went out, I wasn't all too sure I'd be rescued" he said. "Squirrely things go through your mind just as they tell in the Survival Course". Fowler spent 22 hours under freezing conditions without injury except for a broken finger nail. He was rescued by an Ontario Provincial Police Helicopter after being spotted earlier by a Canadian Armed Forces Hercules combing the area with two helicopters.

CASE STUDY B: PANIC SITUATION

A Hornepayne area woman, Agnes Taylor, 33, part-Cree, vanished on a snowy Friday night after leaving her log cabin to set snares for rabbits within sounds of the Trans-Continental CN line. To the bush-wise searchers, her disappearance is equivalent to a city woman getting lost on a trip to the corner drug store.

Despite a volunteer effort on an unprecedented scale, some townspeople are angry more wasn't done. Few say it directly, but it's suggested there'd be more official involvement if a white person were lost instead of an Indian.

One night, the search was called off because of bad weather. Asked if flooding the area with soldiers immediately after Agnes disappeared might have saved her before the weather turned sour, Hornepayne Constable Doug Hamilton said, "That's a good question. I don't know why the Army wasn't called in". How did Agnes Taylor, a big woman at 2m, 90 kg., lose herself within 2 km of the cabin she's known since childhood?

Tracks found by searchers have led some police to resurrect the legend of Bear Walker, the part-man, part-bear of Indian mythology. Agnes's tracks show her suddenly spinning on her heels after walking steadily north away from the rail line. She then went leaping through the tangled bush in the dark - a move with all the sanity of a city dweller jumping in front of a subway train.

Was she frightened, perhaps by a legend that only existed in her mind? Or was she simply a victim of bush fever that strikes even the sanest hunter who suddenly realizes he's lost.

As a child, Agnes would have heard stories of the feared Bear Walker from her father. Even then, she was frightened of the dark and would refuse to go into the bush at night. Yet, her brother Simion, 47, the search leader, scoffs at suggestions the Bear Walker legend played any part in the sudden panic revealed by Agnes' tracks. He prefers to think Agnes' abrupt change of direction was linked to the sound of a passing freight train. Hearing it, she could have made her mad dash through the bush hoping to find the rail track that could have been her life line back to life. In fact, she came within 30 m of the tracks before inexplicably branching off in a new direction.

Shortly afterward, she discarded or lost her sweater and became completely disoriented. Later, searchers found the blue hatchet that was the only weapon Agnes carried in an area dotted by wolf tracks. However,the trail being traced by searchers was made the night of her disappearance. Temperatures fell to about 20 below the next two nights, followed by freezing rain. If she were still alive, they would have been nights of misery for Agnes, clad only in a ski jacket, dark slacks, and rubber boots. One of her relatives, Alex Taylor, 65, says he's seen her in a dream, hunched under a tree - dead.

Whatever happened to Agnes, it marks the first time in years a Hornepayne native has been swallowed up by the bush.

If lost, STOP. Stay put, and don't wander through the bush. Let the rescuers come to you. Members of the search party are friends you haven't met yet.

CASE STUDY C: DEALING WITH DEATH

On May 5, 1979, a small plane carrying Donald Johnson, Brent Dryer, 25, his sister-in-law, Donna Johnson, 50, and the pilot, Norman Pischke, 35, left Estavan, Saskatchewan, bound for Idaho to pick up a puppy from an American dog breeder.

The plane crashed in a remote area of Idaho. Donald Johnson was seriously injured and died 30 hours after the crash. Dryer and his sister-in-law waited by the wreck for a few days with pilot Pischke. No rescuers came, and the pilot decided to make it out on foot. His body was discovered only 2 km from the wreck. In an interview, Dryer is quoted as saying "We talked to God and we prayed...we knew we had to eat him, (Donald Johnson) and we did. We had suffered from hunger for days before deciding to eat the body of her father. We were so damn close to God we knew the man was looked after...he was in peace. I want it known that we weren't ashamed.

"We knew it was right. God told us it was right. We knew it was what Don would have wanted."

Idaho Law does not prohibit the eating of human flesh, therefore the two survivors will likely not be prosecuted. The coroner, Dr. Richard B. Maxwell and sheriff Sid Teugher said they would not confirm the report of cannibalism. Father Walter Wadey of St. John the Baptist Parish in Estavan, mentioned that the reaction by townspeople to the cannibalism incident was subdued and mixed. "As far as most people are concerned, it's a closed matter. There is a reverent silence. We're all glad that the two kids are back but we're sorry that Norman didn't make it."

AN INTERVIEW WITH A SURVIVAL VICTIM

PREAMBLE

While out hunting partridge one September morning, Mr. H. became separated from his partner, and wandered ever deeper into the boreal forest. Not until seven days later did Mr. H. eventually find his way out of the dense bush.

In the meanwhile, the Lakehead Search and Rescue Unit, the Ontario Provincial Police, as well as a host of volunteers, had combed the region for any signs of the young hunter; airplanes, helicopters, and tracking dogs were also used, but to no avail. Ron simply found his way out -- approximately 23 km from his starting point. In an effort to gain an insight into the mental conditions of the wilderness survivor, Dr. Christie and I requested, and received, parental permission to interview Ron H. The following transcript is a verbatim account of the interview.

G. F. Ferri, Co-ordinator,
Lakehead University S & R Program,
Faculty of Outdoor Recreation
Thunder Bay, Ontario

Christie: Your name? age?

Mr. H.:   Ron H., 19 years old.

Christie: Where were you raised?

Mr. H.:   Born in Hamilton, raised in Welland, and moved to Thunder Bay when I was 3.

Christie: What kinds of experiences have you had in the bush?

Mr. H.:   I started hunting 3 years ago; like to spend some time in the bush, and enjoy the wilderness by camping and canoeing.

Christie: Have you had any formal training regarding this matter?

Mr. H.:   No...just the little bit that was available in the Hunter Education course.

Christie:	Have you spent much time in the bush, especially overnight?
Mr. H.:	Yes. I've spent a few overnight camping trips in the wilderness, especially in B.C.
Christie:	Do you have any procedures that you follow when hunting in a new area?
Mr. H.:	I've been out to check the area last year, but not this year...and...I thought I knew it pretty good...so I didn't take along a compass with me. After all, there were some cut trails...these were pretty easy to follow, I thought...
Christie:	In relation to Thunder Bay, where were you lost?
Mr. H.:	I guess about 29 miles down Spruce River road, near the Hicks Lake area.
Christie:	Describe the area.
Mr. H.:	Lots of cut over places...swamps...dense bush...rolling hillside, lots of ridges.
Christie:	Did you ever examine a map of that particular area?
Mr. H.:	No. Not really.
Christie:	Did you carry a compass with you?
Mr. H.:	No. No compass. I usually rely on my hunting partner to have a compass. We keep together. In this case, we became separated, and left the main trail. I thought I knew the trail but it seemed more grown in...it kept getting narrower and narrower...This was actually cleared by moose...it led me to the middle of nowhere...lots of leaves still on the trees...even when I climbed a tree to see where I was I couldn't see because of the ridges. I couldn't see far...I was looking for familiar sights, lakes, smoke, transmitter lines...
Gino:	List all items on your person, especially clothing.
Mr. H.:	I had a pair of workboots on...steel-toed workboots...pair of thick socks...jeans...leather belt with a metal buckle...a set of keys...a green t-shirt...grey sweat shirt...short underwear...a little necklace with a medallion. I had a summer hat, like a baseball cap; six shells and shotgun...

Gino:	Did your boots have laces...?
Mr. H.:	Yes
Gino:	Other items, especially jewelry?
Mr. H.:	Yes, I had this digital watch.
Gino:	Matches?
Mr. H.:	Yes, the paperback kind...they got wet the very first night...
Christie:	When did you realize you were lost?
Mr. H.:	We got out there at 11:30 a.m. on Saturday...were supposed to meet at 2:00 p.m....I kept walking down this trail...By 1:15, I knew I'd be late if I took the trail back, so I decided to go in a straight line across the bush. I wound up in the middle of nowhere an hour later...
Gino:	When did you say to yourself "I'm lost"?
Mr. H.:	In the middle of the bush. I climbed a tree, hopefully to see if I could spot my car...but couldn't see a thing. I jumped down...realized I was lost. I started to panic...jogged around...going to any open clearing...I ran in a complete circle...oddly enough I came right back to the tree I had climbed previously. I saw my footsteps.
Gino:	This is a typical reaction. At what time did you climb the tree?
Mr. H.:	About 2 o'clock.
Gino:	You realized very early that you were lost. In which direction (from the tree) did you travel?
Mr. H.:	To my right.
Gino:	Are you right or left handed?
Mr. H.:	Right handed. I walked in a right, or clockwise, pattern.
Christie:	What did you do then, especially when you came back to the tree?
Mr. H.:	I tried to remember all the stuff I learned...like which direction the moss grows...I was slightly depressed...I tried to remember what people kept telling me what to do, but these thoughts didn't and

wouldn't stay in my mind. Besides, who'd think this would ever happen to me. I didn't pay any attention because I thought I'd never have to use this information, so I never learned it.

Gino: This is a very important comment all people should consider. Kindly repeat it once more.

Mr. H.:   I'd forgotten what I was taught because I really didn't believe this would ever happen to me...I didn't know which direction the sun would set, but I knew generally away from Spruce River Road. So in the afternoon, I followed the sun; in the morning, the sun was to my back...

Gino: When walking, did you follow trails or stick to the high ground?

Mr. H.:   For the first couple of days, I followed the easiest routes...tried to go in straight lines ...even jumped over logs instead of going around them... I was afraid of losing my straight line.

Gino: Your nationality?

Mr. H.:   French-Canadian background.

Gino: When reaching the clearings, were you predominantly travelling uphill, downhill, or on level ground?

Mr. H.:   Mostly on level ground, with some dips...occasionally, I climbed some hills, thinking that just over the next hill would be civilization.

Gino: Did you follow streams, rivers, or other shorelines?

Mr. H.:   Yes, I followed some small streams and a river...I thought it was the Ford river...I kept walking..it became dark, so I decided to build a shelter. Next morning, I couldn't find the river anymore.

Gino: Apparently, you walked most of the time. What made you decide to travel instead of staying put?

Mr. H.:   I always thought that I was close to the road...the wind going through the poplars sounded like highway traffic...so I went further, up the next hill.

Gino: Were these realistic truck sounds? (wind in the trees)

Mr. H.:	While walking, I thought that the highway was just beyond the next hill. I guess I hoped these were truck sounds...
Gino:	What were your emotions and feelings...on a daily basis?
Mr. H.:	I jotted down some notes as soon as I reached the hospital...During the first night ...Saturday...I kept hearing truck sounds...it was raining... walked to a big spruce tree and stayed under this tree. There was a stream, I drank some water. I gathered some kindling and spruce boughs. I layered these around me...started a fire, but it went out because of the rain. I was drenched and decided to lay on the coals. All was soaking wet. I was drenched. The next morning, I decided to start a fire using various methods ...like rubbing 2 sticks together, using my watch, sparking with my metal buckle, igniting the ammunition by stuffing bark in the shells. None worked. I decided to travel.
Gino:	Why did you decide to move?
Mr. H.:	I felt useless just sitting there...wasting time...didn't know if a search was out yet...didn't hear any planes, so I decided to find a highway.
Christie:	What emotions did you feel at this stage?
Mr. H.:	Usually there was a pattern. In the morning I'd be miserable, swearing, and depressed. My injured knee always gave me problems. By 2:00 in the afternoon, I'd be in a better mood...whistling and singing to myself, sometimes conversing with my mind...I felt as if I was on some kind of excursion, proving to myself I could do it...I didn't really see any burdens...everything was peaceful. From the first day I had a partridge, but it went bad by Sunday night so I left it. By Monday morning, I saw a plane go right over me - a bright red plane - cruised directly overhead ...I tried jumping up and down, yelling and screaming...but it went away. I became depressed.
Gino:	For how long?
Mr. H.:	15 to 30 minutes. I sat there for a long time, wondering if they'd ever see me...the trees were so overgrown. I decided to continue walking. It started to get dark. It was hazy (Monday)...so I decided to build another shelter. But the sun was no longer setting in front of me, but behind me; I was cold so I put sides on the shelters to block out the wind. I was shivering and coughing for long periods of time, but still managed to sleep. Everything was now a routine. At 5:00 p.m., I'd start to build a shelter; it was ready by 8:00 p.m. (at dusk). I'd toss and

237

Gino: turn for a while but eventually fell asleep. By 8:00 in the morning, I'd start walking again.

Gino: Did you sleep during the day?

Mr. H.: Sometimes. Only rested periodically. By night, I'd be tired and build another shelter. I'd put boughs under and over me, since it was cold. But when I turned, some of these top boughs fell off. I tried to stay near water as much as possible, drinking when thirsty, even if it tasted skunky.

Gino: Now it's Tuesday...You saw a plane...

Mr. H.: I tried to get the plane's attention. I knew they were looking for me... they were always flying just south of me...I climbed an open tree and sat there...it was freezing, but I saw a helicopter way out in the distance, flying back and forth, but it was heading away from me. I got upset again, ran down the tree...

Gino: What do you mean by upset

Mr. H.: I started to lose hope...that I would never be found...I ran madly towards the noise of the helicopter, but they were getting farther away. I felt panicky when they were leaving me. Up to now I was alright...The feeling was of lost hope, not of being found. I had a gut feeling that if I was to get out, it would be on my own...the brush was too thick to find me...but the planes gave me an inspiration...which...quickly died when they disappeared...So I sat around for a while. It was getting late and over-cast...I was cold...I decided to let them find me. All of a sudden, a bright ray of sunshine hit me in the face...I thought it was a sign for me to follow it, so I did. I came to a swamp, later to a river...both sun and river were going in the same direction...I thought I'd be alright, thinking of myself as an Amazon explorer...

Gino: You were thinking of yourself as an explorer or were you actually exploring the Amazon?

Mr. H.: I was an Amazon explorer at this stage. I followed the river because all explorers were expected to suffer the way I was. The river led me to a swamp, but now the sun was to my back again, so I decided to head into the bush. An hour later, I was back at the same swamp...I had walked in another circle (to my right)...so I decided to stay there. I shot a duck...and laid out my clothes to dry...I was drenched from walking in the river...

Gino:	What parts of the duck did you use?

Gino: What parts of the duck did you use?

Mr. H.: Only the breast. I threw everything else away...I hung the meat out overnight, took a bite, but I couldn't swallow it. By now, I was taking pride in my shelters, adding a roof ...It was getting dark...Suddenly a plane flew directly overhead. I ran into the middle of the swamp... nothing could prevent it from seeing me...I yelled and jumped, firing my gun...I tried to use my watch as a signal...it just kept going, but I thought it went to get the helicopter. By nighttime, nothing happened. I felt that I had to get out on my own. It was now day 5, or Wednesday. I woke up, took a bite of the duck...it tasted disgusting but forced myself to eat 4 bites...I left the rest.

Gino: Did you try to forage for plants?

Mr. H.: Not really...I didn't know too much about plants...I didn't know if they were poisonous or not. I did try a few purple berries...

Christie: Was your mouth chapped?

Mr. H.: Yes, it was.

Gino: Did you notice any colour changes in your urine?

Mr. H.: Yes, initially it was a light yellow...a few days later, it was much darker. I was urinating (day 5) 2 or 3 times daily...I had the runs constantly... used moss to dry myself.

Gino: What did you do on Wednesday?

Mr. H.: I found a dirt road...followed it in one direction for a few hours, but led nowhere; I followed it in the opposite direction, towards the setting sun. It led me to a river. I left the road and followed the river for the rest of the day. It was getting dark so I decided to build a shelter... between 2 fallen trees...it reminded me of a coffin...

Gino: Why did you use the term "coffin"?

Mr. H.: It seemed comfortable, like a coffin, with sides and a roof. That night I had some weird dreams...that I had a walkie-talkie and talking to the airplanes, who brought some friends to see me. These guys eventually left, and asked me to come with them, but I wouldn't ...I woke up...it was so real...I was in my shelter but all of my friends were leaving. I couldn't leave. I thought this was a symbol...that my soul was being taken away but it didn't want to go. Next morning I was very depressed...it felt that my mind was wandering ...thinking that, when found, perhaps I didn't want to go . My dreams started to confuse me. This was on day 6 (Thursday). I felt delirious.

Gino: Let's go back to the dreams. Any signs of animals in your dreams.

Mr. H.:   Not really.

Gino: Parents?

Mr. H.:   They were never part of my dreams, although I thought of them during the day an awful lot. Mostly my friends were in my dreams.

Gino: Let's talk about Thursday (day 6). What was going through your mind?

Mr. H.:   I was cold all the time...always following the sun, but it never got me anywhere; I decided to follow a blasting sound I'd heard for a few days ...but I thought it could be tricks on my mind...The sounds did not come at a regular interval. I climbed a ridge, and found a trapper's trail...found a small lake...went around it and found a leg-hold trap... kept thinking that I'd meet the trapper, who'd tell me there was no way out...that he'd been lost...lost for years. It started to drizzle and to rain. I stopped to dry out my socks. I climbed a tree and kept hearing these blasting sounds...more like highway sounds... the kind I'd been hearing since the beginning. I decided to follow the sounds. At night, I made a shelter, but went out to listen if the sounds (highway) were real...they were becoming more real every minute. I decided to get a good night's rest and find the highway. Next morning, I climbed a tree, heard the sounds, and headed towards them.

Gino: Could these have been mental tricks?

Mr. H.:   Maybe. This was happening all along. Suddenly, I found a large lake (Hicks), with some camps. I knew I was close to the highway...I found another trail...but headed through the bush to the lake. I went around the lake towards the highway sound (Friday). I soon found it, and started hitchhiking.

Gino: Let's go back to the bush. You mentioned some methods of keeping warm at night...

Mr. H.:   Yes, at night I piled lots of boughs above and below me...but the ones on top kept falling off when I turned. I didn't have a roof on the shelters.

Gino: How often were you drinking?

Mr. H.: Almost every opportunity I had...I knew I was getting weaker because, in the beginning I was keeping up a fast pace; later, I could feel myself dragging through the bush. It was a burden and no longer exciting. By the last day, I was very tired. My legs had to be massaged; they were cramped...

Gino: What mistakes do you feel you made out there?

Mr. H.: Not following the sun consistently, and perhaps not carrying a compass and maps...

Gino: Did it ever dawn on you to stay put?

Mr. H.: Quite a few times. But after an hour or so of sitting, I'd get bored and feel that I was wasting my time...sitting there rotting...I knew I'd have to find the way out on my own ...the airplanes had failed me...

Gino: You saw planes almost every day, if I'm not mistaken...

Mr. H.: Yes...

Gino: If by your experiences, you could offer some suggestions to others, what would they be?

Mr. H.: Perhaps, get some training about the bush...know the area...have a compass...map...waterproof matches...bright balloon...

Gino: You mentioned training. What kind of training?

Mr. H.: How to find your way in the bush if lost...some knowledge of edible plants...signs for direction finding...wilderness survival training...

Christie: What about preparations before heading for the bush?

Mr. H.: Tell someone exactly where you're going...know the area.

Gino: A lot of folks seem to think that this kind of thing can't happen to them. Any comments?

Mr. H.: I had this feeling...even some that know the area think that it can't possibly happen...

Gino: Describe your physical condition after 7 days in the bush.

Mr. H.:   I'd lost 17 pounds...was slightly dehydrated...lost a lot of potassium... my feet were frostbitten. These swelled like balloons at the hospital. They fed me intravenously for 2 days...

Christie: Were you aware you had frostbitten feet?

Mr. H.:   No...they felt soft, wet, prudish, and wrinkled, mostly because I always made my shelter too small and they always stuck out. I kept my boots on at night. The last night was by far the coldest...I don't know how much longer I could have lasted...

PROJECT STOP: AIDING THE LOST YOUNGSTER

A. PREAMBLE

A number of years ago, a nine-year old boy disappeared while hiking with his family through a tract of dense, wilderness bush land. Following a four-day search, he was found dead of exposure. Apparently, the youngster wandered aimlessly through forest and swamps in a futile effort to find his way to safety. Unfortunately, he walked out of the initial search area, with tragic results.

This programme is aimed at teaching youngsters what to do if lost in a wilderness environment. The name of the programme is based on its primary message: if lost, stay put, STOP, until help arrives. This concept, surprisingly, is difficult for many to comprehend and to accept; many novices believe that one should somehow find his/her way out of the bush. However, the basic philosophical platform of the National Association for Search and Rescue Organizations, and most wilderness survival instructors, is to remain in one spot and wait for searchers.

One cannot over-emphasize this message...staying put is the single most important decision a great number of lost individuals must make. Many children (and adults) panic when lost; they run great distances; get overheated; strip off and loosen clothing. Some youngsters hide from searchers for fear of punishment when found. Remaining stationary prevents one's wanton self-destructive habit of wasting calories caused by unnecessary movements. It also enables local search and rescue units to focus their attention on one specific geographic area, an area made considerably larger should the lost person wander aimlessly throughout the wilderness.

Due to our unique location, surrounded by lakes, rivers, and forests, we should at least introduce Project STOP to some students.

Many experienced individuals, working in harmony with teachers, administrators, Ministry of Natural Resources personnel, Search and Rescue officials, as well as with interested members of the general community at large, would be more than willing to talk to children regarding the Project.

Geared primarily for groups of elementary and high school students, the programme could be tailored to suit the specific age being addressed. A proposed slide presentation, lasting anywhere from 15 minutes to half-day sessions (depending on the age level, student involvement, and time restraints), could include a number of preventative, survival, and rescue suggestions, including:

i) making yourself big: wave a T-shirt or constructing a big "X" of branches on the ground, or stamping one in the snow; and lying down flat when hearing a plane, thereby making oneself more visible from the air, keeping in mind that this should be done in an open area.

ii) when camping or hiking in wooded areas, individuals should carry a whistle and a large trash-can liner with a small face-hole cut in front. Although children are taught never to pull a piece of plastic over their heads, the proper use of a garbage bag with a face-hole affords great insulation and might prevent death from exposure if lost overnight.

iii) other tips include how to keep bugs from biting; where and how to set up distress signals and how a search party operates.

Should any organization decide to accept, develop, and adopt this programme, it may someday save a child's life. And that's a sobering thought!

B. PROJECT STOP

Although this project had its genesis in the south-western regions of the United States, it can be re-designed, re-structured, and refined to suit the unique geographic features of any part of Canada.

Some alterations have to be made. For example, water conservation principles, although critical in the dry regions of the U.S., are not as vital and applicable to, let us say, northern Ontario.

I. Implementation: The Instructor (s)

As was previously mentioned, this Project takes the form of a guided discussion-slide presentation format; however, prior to addressing the group of youngsters, the leader responsible for the children is to meet and discuss the curriculum content with the individual(s) responsible for presenting the Project. In so doing, all parties concerned will know why, how, when and what is involved; furthermore, when an outsider is warmly welcomed and introduced to young (and old) children, (s)he, and his/her ideas and comments stand a greater chance of becoming accepted, and remembered, by a captive audience. Also, we encourage others to attend the presentation, including parents and community members, since their support is needed if the Project is to succeed.

Finally, participants should be advised that we are adhering to the "Stay-put, stay-found" philosophy.

Only in the extreme conditions will the child be cautioned to wander through the wilderness. If travel is necessary, it should be restricted to limited distances only. Reasons for this philosophy will be given throughout the entire presentation.

II. Implementation: The Students

The presentation commences with a short, true story. Once the class has been introduced to the speaker, (s)he immediately commences with the story: Let's talk about a real-life event that happened not too long ago, and not far from here. A young boy, during a fishing trip, decided to take a short cut through the woods. He finally reached the river. Wearing only a light shirt, jeans, and running shoes, he discovered that although the fish were not biting, the bugs surely were. He nonetheless remained a little longer. (He did let his parents know where he was going, and how long he'd be fishing).

Eventually, feeling a little hungry, he decided to go home. In order to save time (it's getting a little dark), he looks for the short cut. Leaving the well-beaten trail, he heads into the forest. Soon, it's totally dark. Still no sign of the river or the road. The boy is lost! He starts to walk faster, then to run, but he doesn't come any closer to home. He's very frightened. He sits down under a large tree, curls up into a ball, and closes his eyes...he's late for supper...mom and dad will be wondering where he might be. They're not angry, only concerned.

Early next morning, the young boy is still under the same tree. He hasn't moved. Eventually, he hears someone calling his name. Listening carefully, he again hears his name. He yells back! A search party has found him...cold, tired, frightened, and badly bitten by bugs. Accepting food given to him by searchers, he's taken home, hugged, and welcomed by his parents.

III. Guided Discussion: On Being Prepared

Using slides where and whenever applicable, the speaker, through questioning, attempts to draw the following information from the class:

i) some mistakes made by the boy during the fishing trip:

- wearing inappropriate clothing,
- leaving pathway,
- staying too long (getting dark),
- running in the darkness,
- not bringing a lunch or extra clothing,
- not wearing a watch.

ii) correct steps followed by the boy:

- informing his parents as to where he was going, resulting in the search taking place in the right vicinity.
- remaining stationary for the night and day.
- curling up into a ball at night.
- replying to the searchers' voices and accepting their food.
- understanding his parent's feelings: they weren't angry, only concerned for his safety.

Answers are written on chalkboard, with an appropriate verbal explanation for each reply. For example, remaining stationary enabled the searchers to locate the boy much sooner than had he wandered throughout the wilderness.

Incidentally, students, in understanding the searchers' role, may accept them as friends and not as strangers. These concepts will be repeated throughout the presentation. A guided discussion leads students to understanding what (and why) certain items should be carried whenever trekking through the forest. These include the following:

i) bandaids,
ii) some food: dried fruit, nuts, sandwiches,
iii) whistle,
iv) extra clothing: long pants, pull-over jacket,
v) water container and water,
vi) matches (waterproof),
vii) raincoat; large plastic garbage bag,
viii) insect repellent

Answers, along with explanations, are written on the chalkboard. All items carried serve some purpose; it is imperative that children understand their purpose. For example, why is a raincoat necessary? This might be accomplished (using the raincoat as an example) through guided questioning and story telling:

How many have been caught in the rain without a raincoat? It's nice and sunny in the morning, but your parents urge you to take along rainwear. You don't! On the way to your favourite fishing spot, it begins to pour. You should have brought the raincoat. Besides, even if it doesn't rain, why not use this extra clothing as a blanket or pillow? Suggest to students how the items they're carrying (ie. raincoat) serve more than one function. How can a plastic garbage bag be used? Demonstrate to students the proper method of utilization, (as well as other uses: ie. additional rainwear; carrying items-extra knapsack; wrapping fish; and blanket).

The gear any person decides to take on a trip should be kept together in a small knapsack. Everything is close together and easily carried. Besides, it's a lot more fun to walk without dragging sweaters or jackets; also, your hands are free.

In any case, one point should always be stressed: before leaving, students are to inform their parents and friends of their destination and return time; also, the knapsack is to be carried whenever venturing out of the city.

IV. S.T.O.P.

Remind students of the initial story...how the boy ran through the woods. Again, through guided discussion and questioning, and using slides when appropriate, spend some time to explain fear and panic, and how these feelings can and must be controlled. Fear begins when the individual realizes he's lost and doesn't know where he is; furthermore, this emotion lasts until he's found. How can it be controlled?

Guided discussion in story-telling fashion, encourage children to sit down and admit to themselves that they're lost, and not to wander any further. Introduce class to the S.T.O.P. concept: Security, Think, Observe, and Plan.

Writing each heading on the chalkboard, a series of concepts are developed, illustrated, and stressed. These include:

1. Security

    i)   One of the best ways of controlling fear and panic is to seek security; become friends with an object...hug a live tree or a rock; give it a name.

    ii)   Trees are not lost and make good friends:
           - they listen to you
           - they don't talk back
           - they even provide some shelter from rain

    iii)   Stay close to your new friends; think of your parents, that someone will be looking for you; tell all this to your new friends.

When hiking through the bush, always travel with a buddy.

2. Think

    i)   Think about what we're telling you right now. It may come in handy some day.

    ii)   It's natural to feel cold, scared, and hungry when lost, but think of your family; besides, people are now looking for you; you'll soon be found; your parents want you home as soon as possible.

    iii)   It's best to stay put under your tree, in a dry spot; searchers, and other friends are looking for you; your parents want you home safe and sound. They're not angry, only concerned about your safety.

    iv)   The tree, and nature, won't hurt you but they're not going to help unless you think...how can branches be used to keep warm? What other plants are useful? Stress full use of trees and plants, including possible shelter and food. List some examples.

3. Observe

    i)   Keep eyes and ears open for those searchers who are presently looking for you.

    ii)   Shelter and comfort is available under a conifer tree. Break some boughs for bedding. Be careful of sharp branches...they can and will hurt you.

    iii)   Keep away from possibly dangerous areas such as swamps, cliffs, fast-flowing rivers, and wet or damp areas.

    iv)   Once a friendly high and dry tree comes to greet you, stay with him and make yourself comfortable; if possible, make yourself visible from every direction.

4. Plan

    i)   Put on extra clothing before darkness sets in. Use the garbage container as a sleeping bag, and roll up into a ball. Demonstrate T-shirt over head technique.

ii)   Make certain a bough bedding is under you; use the raincoat as a blanket; stay under your tree - nice and dry. Keep away from low-lying swamps and bogs. Plan to stay comfortable until searchers find you.

iii)   Plan on seeing mom and dad very soon...they're waiting for you.

5. Getting Found

Although there is no set way of getting found, the lost person can assist searchers. Don't hide! A person searching for you is a friend you haven't met yet. Blow your whistle occasionally, three blasts...to attract attention. Three is your lucky number - it's a distress signal - anything in threes will certainly attract attention from the ground and from the air. List examples:

- triangles
- piling rocks
- three fires

Back home, your parents are worried, but not angry...they love you; therefore, there is no need to hide from anyone looking for you. On the contrary, keep eyes and ears open for the searchers.

Through guided discussion, lead students to the methods a lost person could use to attract searchers:

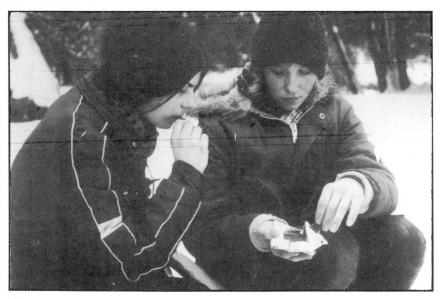

Carry an extra supply of food on you. When hungry, stop, eat, and relax.

i)   listen for airplanes, people, and tracking dogs,

ii)   if hearing a plane, wave brightly coloured clothing while lying down in an open area. Be as big as a house. Demonstrate.

iii)   make nature different by breaking branches, rock piling, and overturning plants (in threes). Demonstrate.

iv)   urinate near the trees to attract the tracking dogs.

These actions will help the searchers to find you.

6. Staying Found: Summary

Individuals presenting Project STOP can now summarize by asking students to re-tell the initial story. With the information they now have, ask class what gear they should take on a trip. How could they keep from getting lost? Also, what would they do if lost? Write students' answer on chalkboard. Also review the following points:

i)   Before leaving, inform family and friends as to where going and when returning. Return on time.

ii)   Check the weather forecast.

iii)   Bring along knapsack with proper gear.

iv)   Stay on path-way; do what you planned on doing.

v)   Return before darkness sets in. Keep track of time.

vi)   If large, man-made objects (radio towers, smoke stacks, silos) are visible, keep them in sight if at all possible.

We strongly encourage all individuals to follow these suggestions. Perhaps some time could be devoted to describing the unique geographic characteristics of this region, and how it can be a beautiful, but dangerous place. Needless to say, some time is devoted to answering questions. Use this opportunity to list, once again, those preventative aspects stressed by Project STOP.

FIVE MENTAL STAGES OF THE LOST VICTIM

The inability of the average person to retain a record of his/her itinerary to the rear, while (s)he selects his/her route ahead, is more than likely responsible for more loss of life in the woods than any other single factor.

I The lost individual blindly obeys that uncontrollable impulse to run madly, tearing, through the underbrush regardless of clothing, or exposed skin, so as to get as far from the hateful spot as possible. (S)he does not admit (s)he's lost.

II Eventually, (s)he will wander hopelessly on, sometimes in circles, at times within measurable distance of friends, past spots with which (s)he is familiar, but is no longer in a condition to recognize.

III Ultimately, the mind becomes obsessed by strange images: birds, become spirits; rotting stumps, become animals; the owl, floating soundlessly, is an apparition. The whole world of trees and shadows are now dark labyrinths, and (s)he's possessed by a dread that no known danger of ordinary experiences could possibly account for.

IV   Now in a fevered, weakened condition, (s)he becomes the victim of hallucinations, and is beset by a form of insanity, the "madness of the woods" (a form of sensory deprivation). The environment assumes the shape of a tomb. This madness is all-encompassing; (s)he is engulfed in the typical psychosis of the lost victim syndrome! Under the influences of this psychosis, the person will doubt compass readings, question all known facts (eg. sun's direction) and fail to recognize places with which (s)he is very familiar; as well the victim might run away from rescuers.

V Once this mental state is reached, (s)he presumably stumbles on, muttering and raving; falling, getting up, only to fall again, crawling at last in the resistless urge to keep on while there is yet still life. Ahead, just ahead, that sense of hope, never fulfilled. Death is close by!

SUGGESTED READING

Boy Scouts of America. *Fieldbook for Boys & Men.* BSA, 1967.

Brittain, Wm. *Survival Outdoors.* New York: Monarch Press, 1977.

Brower, D.R., ed. *The Sierra Club Wilderness Handbook.* Ballantine, 1967.

Chassler, S. "School for Survival". *Collier's*, 1951, 128(23): 24-25.

Doucette, E. "Terror in the Woods". *Coronet*, 1950, 29 (1): 134-137.

Greenbank, A. " Could You Survive?" *Outdoor Life*, 1969, 143(4): 90-93.

Klaben, H., with B. Day. *Hey, I'm Alive*. McGraw-Hill, 1964.

Kobalenko, J. "Surviving". *Outdoor Canada*, May, 1990 48-62.

Montana State University. *Winter Survival*. Cooperative Extension Services, 1970.

Mulling, R.J., as told to Ben East, "Lost for Forty Days". *Outdoor Life*, 1954, 113(5): 36-37.

Nordic World Magazine. *Winter Safety Handbook*. Mountain View: World Publications, 1975.

Politano, C. *Child Survival. Lost in the Woods.* Sidney: Porthole Press, 1984.

Risk, P.H. "Lost Children Can Survive if We Stop Scaring Them to Death". *Michigan Natural Resources*, July/August 1976.

Rogers, E.L. "A Saga of Survival". *Field & Stream,* 1969, 74(2): 78-79, 118-121.

Schiller, P. "No Word for Luck." *Outside Magazine*. Nov. 1982, 63-68.

Stewart, A. *Ordeal by Hunger*. New York: Pocket Books.

ABOUT THE AUTHOR

Gino F. Ferri, Ph.D., is the director of Survival in the Bush, Inc., a company which acts as an instructional and consulting firm for groups of educators, students, hunters, anglers, executives, outdoor leaders, and others interested in mastering any number of wilderness survival skills. At Humber College of Applied Arts and Technology in Toronto, Canada, he has established a year-round wilderness survival programme. Gino has travelled extensively in the Canadian Northlands, and has taught survival techniques to Inuit, Metis, and Native People. He has written two manuals: *Wilderness Survival*, and *Eating Out*, a unit of edible wild plants. At the present, he is researching the reaction patterns of victims lost or stranded in the wilderness.

Gino also wrote for *Angler and Hunter*, *Leisure World*, and *The Canadian Hunting and Shooting* magazines; topic: wilderness survival.